# Ḍarūrat-ul-Imam

# The Need for the Imam

## ḤAḌRAT MIRZA GHULAM AHMAD OF QADIAN
The Promised Messiah and Mahdi[as]
Founder of the Ahmadiyya Muslim Jamāʿat

ISLAM INTERNATIONAL PUBLICATIONS LIMITED

ضرورة الامام

# The Need for the Imam
**English Translation of** *Ḍarūrat-ul-Imam*
written in Urdu by Ḥaḍrat Mirza Ghulam Ahmad of
Qadian[as], in 1898, many Urdu editions published since.

First English Translation published in UK, 2007
Present Edition (UK), 2009

Published by:
Islam International Publications Ltd
Islamabad
Sheephatch Lane
Tilford, Surrey
United Kingdom GU10 2AQ


Printed in UK at:
Raqeem Press
'Islamabad'
Tilford, Surrey GU10 2AQ

Cover Design: Adnan Rashid


ISBN: 1-85372-761-X

# About the Author

Born in 1835 in Qadian (India), Ḥaḍrat Mirza Ghulam Ahmad, the Promised Messiah and Mahdi[as], remained dedicated to the study of the Holy Quran and to a life of prayer and devotion. Finding Islam the target of foul attacks from all directions, the fortunes of Muslims at a low ebb, faith yielding to doubt and religion only skin-deep, he undertook vindication and exposition of Islam. In his vast corpus of writings (including his epoch-making *Brāhīn-e-Ahmadiyya*), his lectures, discourses, religious debates etc., he argued that Islam was a living faith and the only faith by following which man could establish contact with his Creator and enter into communion with Him. The teachings contained in the Holy Quran and the Law promulgated by Islam were designed to raise man to moral, intellectual and spiritual perfection. He announced that God had appointed him the Messiah and Mahdi as mentioned in the prophecies of the Bible, the Holy Quran and *Aḥādīth*. In 1889 he began to accept initiation into his Community which is now established in one hundred and seventy six countries. His eighty books are written mostly in Urdu, but some are in Arabic and Persian.

After his demise in 1908, the Promised Messiah[as] was succeeded by Ḥaḍrat Maulawī Nūr-ud-Dīn[ra], Khalīfatul

Masīḥ I. On the death of Ḥaḍrat Maulawī Nūr-ud-Dīn[ra] in 1914, Ḥaḍrat Mirza Bashīr-ud-Dīn Mahmood Ahmad[ra], who was also the Promised Messiah's[as] Promised Son, was elected as Khalīfa. Ḥaḍrat Mirza Bashīr-ud-Dīn Mahmood Ahmad[ra] remained in office for nearly fifty two years. He died in 1965 and was succeeded by his eldest son, Ḥaḍrat Hafiz Mirza Nasir Ahmad[rh], the Promised grandson of the Promised Messiah[as]. After seventeen years of meritorious services he passed away in 1982. He was succeeded by his younger brother, Ḥaḍrat Mirza Tahir Ahmad[rh] as Khalīfatul Masīḥ IV who, having led the Community to its present strength and global recognition, passed away on the 19th April, 2003. Ḥaḍrat Mirza Masroor Ahmad Khalīfatul Masīḥ V[at] is the present head of the Community and enjoys the distinction of being the great-grandson of Ḥaḍrat Mirza Ghulam Ahmad[as].

# Table of Contents

# Foreword

Ḥaḍrat Mirza Ghulam Ahmad (1835-1908), the holy founder of the world-wide Ahmadiyya Muslim Jamāʻat, born in Qadian, a village in rural Punjab, India, was the Divinely appointed Reformer of the latter days and the Promised Messiah and Mahdi. He was sent by God in fulfilment of the prophecies contained in the Holy Bible, the Holy Quran and Hadith, with the express task of rediscovering Islam in its pristine purity and beauty, and bringing mankind back to the Creator.

*Ḍarūrat-ul-Imam*, or *The Need for the Imam*, spells out in depth the urgency and need for the Imam of the age, and his qualities and hallmarks as the Divinely appointed guide, the voice articulate of the age, and the constant recipient of Divine revelations, and how all these qualities are fully present in the person of the holy author.

The earlier English translation from Urdu was done by Qadi Abdul Hamid Sahib, of blessed memory. The present edition has been revised by Wakalat Tasnif, Rabwah.

I am grateful to Sahibzada Mirza Anas Ahmad Sahib, Wakīlul Ishāʻat, Taḥrīk-e-Jadīd, Rabwah, and Maulana Muniruddin Shams Sahib, Additional Wakīlut Taṣnīf, London, for their valuable suggestions and their help in bringing out this book. I am also indebted to the following who assisted me in the various stages of this project:
Dhulqarnain, Azizur Rahman Hafiz-Zada, Raja Ata-ul-Mannan, Syed Tanwir Mujtaba, Usman Ahmad Ghumman, Kashif Imran Khalid, Tahir Mahmood Mubashar

Chaudhry Muhammad Ali
Wakīlut Taṣnīf,
Taḥrīk-e-Jadīd, Rabwah
January 14th 2007

# Publishers' Note

Please note that the words in the text in normal brackets ( ) and in between the long dashes—are the words of the Promised Messiah[as] and if any explanatory words or phrases are added by the translator for the purpose of clarification, they are put in square brackets [ ].

The name of Muhammad[sa], the Holy Prophet of Islam, has been followed by the symbol [sa], which is an abbreviation for the salutation *Ṣallallāhu 'Alaihi Wasallam* (may peace and blessings of Allah be upon him). The names of other Prophets and Messengers are followed by the symbol [as], an abbreviation for *'Alaihissalām* (on whom be peace). The actual salutations have not generally been set out in full, but they should nevertheless, be understood as being repeated in full in each case. The symbol [ra] is used with the name of the companions of the Holy Prophet[sa] and those of the Promised Messiah[as]. It stands for *Raḍī Allāhu 'anhu/'anha/'anhum* (May Allah be pleased with him/with her/with them). Symbol [rh] stands for *Rahimahullāhu Ta'ālā* (may Allah have mercy on him). Symbol [at] stands for *Ayyadahullāhu Ta'ālā* (May Allah, the Mighty help him).

In transliterating Arabic words we have followed the following system adopted by the Royal Asiatic Society.

ا      at the beginning of a word, pronounced as *a, i, u* preceded by a very slight aspiration, like *h* in the English word 'honour'.

ث      *th*, pronounced like th in the English word 'thing'.

ح      *ḥ*, a guttural aspirate, stronger than h.

خ      *kh*, pronounced like the Scotch ch in 'loch'.

ذ     *dh*, pronounced like the English th in 'that'.

ص     ṣ, strongly articulated s.

ض     ḍ, similar to the English th in 'this'.

ط     ṭ, strongly articulated palatal t.

ظ     ẓ, strongly articulated z.

ع     ', a strong guttural, the pronunciation of which must be learnt by the ear.

غ *gh*, a sound approached very nearly in the r '*grasseye*' in French, and in the German r. It requires the muscles of the throat to be in the 'gargling' position whilst pronouncing it.

ق     *q*, a deep guttural k sound.

ئ     ', a sort of catch in the voice.

**Short vowels are represented by:**

*a*    for ───ˊ─── (like *u* in 'bud');

*i*    for ─────── (like *i* in 'bid');

*u*    for ───ˋ─── (like *oo* in 'wood');

**Long vowels by:**

*ā*    for ───ˊ─── or آ (like *a* in 'father');

*ī*    for ی ─────── or ─────── (like *ee* in 'deep');

*ū*    for و ───ˋ─── (like *oo* in 'root');

**Other:**

*ai*    for ی ───ˊ─── (like *i* in 'site')*;

*au*    for و ───ˊ─── (resembling *ou* in 'sound').

Please note that in transliterated words the letter 'e' is to be pronounced as in 'prey' which rhymes with 'day'; however the pronunciation is flat without the element of English diphthong.

---

* In Arabic words like شیخ (Shaikh) there is an element of diphthong which is missing when the word is pronounced in Urdu.

If in Urdu and Persian words 'e' is lengthened a bit more it is transliterated as 'ei' to be pronounced as 'ei' in 'feign' without the element of diphthong thus 'کے' is transliterated as 'Kei'. For the nasal sound of 'n' we have used the symbol 'ṅ'. Thus Urdu word 'میں' is transliterated as 'meiṅ'.

The consonants not included in the above list have the same phonetic value as in the principal languages of Europe.

We have not transliterated Arabic words which have become part of English language, e.g., Islam, Mahdi, Quran[**], Hijra, Ramadan, Hadith, ulema, umma, sunna, kafir, pukka etc.

For quotes straight commas (straight quotes) are used to differentiate them from the curved commas used in the system of transliteration, ' for ع, ' for ء. Commas as punctuation marks are used according to the normal usage. Similarly for apostrophe normal usage is followed.

**Publishers**

---

[*] These transliterations are not included in the system of transliteration by Royal Asiatic Society.

[**] Concise Oxford Dictionary records Quran in three forms— Quran, Qur'an and Koran.

xi

# The Facsimile of the Title of the First Edition

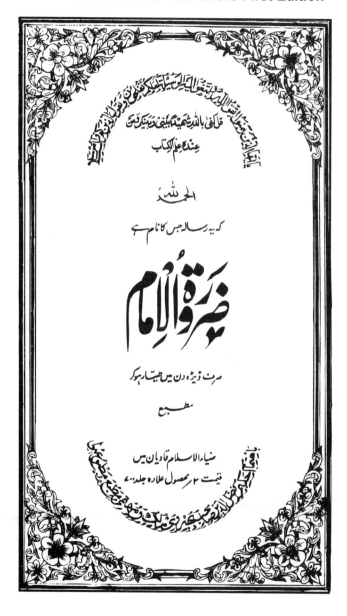

[Translation of the Title Page]

*O ye who believe! fear Allah and seek the way of approach unto*
*Him and strive in His way that you may prosper.*
*And those who disbelieve say, 'Thou art not a Messenger.'*
*Say, 'Sufficient is Allah as a Witness between me and you and*
*so is he who possesses knowledge of the Book. '*

All praise belongs to Allah, that this book entitled

# *Ḍarūrat-ul-Imam*
[The Need for the Imam]

was written in only one and a half day
and printed at
Ḍiyā'-ul-Islam Press, Qadian,
under the supervision of Hakim Faḍl-ud-Dīn Bhervi,
the owner and manager of the press.

بِسْمِ اللهِ الرَّحْمٰنِ الرَّحِيْمِ [1]

اَلْحَمْدُ لِلّٰهِ وَ سَلَامٌ عَلٰى عِبَادِهِ الَّذِيْنَ اصْطَفٰى [2]

# Ḍarūrat-ul-Imam
## The Need for the Imam

Now, then, let it be clear that an authentic Hadith[3] testifies that he who does not recognize the Imam of his

---

[1] In the name of Allah, the Gracious, the Merciful. [Publishers]

[2] All praise belongs to Allah, and peace be upon His chosen servants. [Publishers]

حَـدثـنـا عبد الله حدثنى ابى حدثنا اَسْوَدُ بْنُ عَامِرٍ انا اَبُوبَكْرٍ عَنْ عاصم عن أبى

صَـالِـح عَنْ مُعَاوِيَةَ قَالَ قَالَ رَسُوْلُ اللهِ صَلَّى اللهُ عَلَيْهِ وَسَلَّمْ مَنْ مَاتَ بِغَيْرِ اِمَامٍ

مَـاتَ مِيْتَةً جَـاهِلِيَّةً صفحه ٩٦ جلد ٤ مسند احمد و اخرجه احمد و الترمذى

و ابـن خـزيـمة و ابـن حبان و صححه من حديث الحارث الاشعرى بلفظ مَنْ

مَـاتَ وَ لَيْـسَ عَلَيْـهِ اِمَـامُ جَـمَـاعَةٍ فَـاِنَّ مَوْتَهٗ مَوْتَةً جَاهِلِيَّةً ورواه الحاكم من

حَـديـثِ بـن عـمـرو مـن حـديـث معاوية و رواه البزّار من حديث ابن عباس[3]

[Author]

*Translation:* Abdullah related to us from his father, he from Aswad bin Amir, he from Abu Bakr, he from Asim, he from Abu Salih, and he from Muawiyah, that the Holy Prophet[sa] said: 'He who dies without [recognizing] the Imam dies the death of ignorance.' Page 96 vol. 4 *Musnad Ahmad.* This [Hadith] is also recorded by Ahmad, Tirmidhī, Ibn-e-Khuzaimah and Ibni Habban. Al-Harith Al-Ashari gives another version of this Hadith: 'He who dies without [following] the Imam of a Jamā'at certainly dies a death of ignorance.' Ḥākim reports this from Bin Amr, he from Muawiyah, he from Bazzar, and he from Ibni Abbas. [Publishers]

1

time, dies the death of ignorance. This Hadith is enough to make the heart of a righteous man seek after the Imam of the age, for to die in ignorance is such a great misfortune that no evil or ill-luck lies outside its scope. Therefore, in keeping with this testament of the Holy Prophet<sup>sa</sup>, it becomes incumbent upon every seeker after truth to persist in his quest for the true Imam.

It is wrong to suppose that anyone who experiences a true dream, or for whom the door of Divine revelation opens, can be called an Imam. On the contrary, to be an Imam requires a comprehensive condition and a perfect and absolute [spiritual] state because of which he is designated Imam in heaven. Obviously no one can be called Imam merely on account of righteousness and piety. God Almighty says:

$$ \text{وَاجْعَلْنَا لِلْمُتَّقِيْنَ اِمَامًا} ^4 $$

If every righteous person was to be considered an Imam, all the believers who are righteous would automatically become Imams, and this would be in direct conflict with the purport of this verse. Similarly, according to the clear textual authority of the Holy Quran, not every recipient of revelation or anyone who experiences true dreams can be considered

---

<sup>4</sup> ... and make *each of* us a leader of the righteous.—*Al-Furqān*, 25: 75 [Publishers]

an Imam, for these have already been promised to ordinary believers:

$$\text{لَهُمُ الْبُشْرٰى فِي الْحَيٰوةِ الدُّنْيَا (10/65)}^{5}$$

That is to say, in this very world the believers will be blessed with true dreams and revelations. Again the Holy Quran says:

$$\text{اِنَّ الَّذِيْنَ قَالُوْا رَبُّنَا اللهُ ثُمَّ اسْتَقَامُوْا}$$

$$\text{تَتَنَزَّلُ عَلَيْهِمُ الْمَلٰٓئِكَةُ اَلَّا تَخَافُوْا وَلَا تَحْزَنُوْا}^{6}$$

That is to say, those who believe in Allah and then remain steadfast, it is to them that angels continue to communicate revelations of glad tidings and comfort them, just as the mother[7] of Moses[as] was comforted through Divine revelation. The Holy Quran, however, shows that revelations or dreams of this kind are spiritual gifts to the ordinary believers whether they are men or women. The fact that they are the recipients of such revelations does not mean that they no longer need the Imam of the age. More often than not, such revelations concern only their own persons and do not convey any [spiritual] knowledge, nor do they carry great conviction. Indeed many of them are not fit to be

---

[5] *Yūnus*, 10: 65 [Publishers]
[6] *Ḥā Mīm Al-Sajdah*, 41: 31 [Publishers]
[7] *Al-Qaṣaṣ*, 28:8 [Publishers]

relied upon. On the other hand, such revelations sometimes cause one to stumble. And until spiritual
knowledge is conveyed through the guidance of the
Imam, one is not immune to such dangers. An example
of this can be found in early Islam: A scribe of the
Holy Quran, who, by virtue of being close to the Prophetic light, would often partake of the revelation of
Quranic verses just as the Imam—the Holy Prophet[sa]—
was going to dictate it. One day the scribe thought to
himself, 'What difference is there between me and the
Holy Prophet[sa]? I too receive Divine revelation!' This
thinking led him to his ruin. It is recorded that even
his grave threw him out, quite like Balaam[8] who was
similarly ruined. Ḥaḍrat Umar[ra9] too was the recipient
of Divine revelation, but he regarded himself unwor-
thy and had no ambition to be a partner in the True
Imāmat established on earth by the God of Heaven.
Rather, he considered himself to be a humble ser-
vant. The Grace of God, therefore, made him the
vicegerent of the True Imāmat. Uwais Qarni[ra] was
recipient of Divine, was also the recipient of revelation. He was so humble that he thought it

---

[8] A learned man among the Israelites. (Num. 31:16, 2Pet. 2:15)
[Publishers]
[9] 'Umar ibn Al-Khaṭṭāb (r. 634-644), the second Rightly
Guided Caliph. [Publishers]

disrespectful even to present himself before the Sun of Prophethood and Imāmat. Our master, the Holy Prophet Muhammad<sup>sa</sup>, would often turn his face towards Yemen, and say:

اَجِدُ رِیْحَ الرَّحْمٰنِ مِنْ قِبَلِ الْیَمَنِ

That is 'I smell the sweet fragrance of the Beneficent One coming from Yemen'. This was an allusion to the fact that Uwais was indeed the recipient of Divine light. It is a pity, however, that most people of this age do not realize the need for True Imāmat. By experiencing a solitary true dream or a few words of revelation, they come to imagine that they have no need for the Imam of the time. 'Are we any less?' [They seem to suggest]. They do not realize that such a thought is altogether sinful because our Holy Prophet<sup>sa</sup> has testified to the need for an Imam for every century. He has clearly said that whoever returns to God Almighty, without having recognized the Imam of his age, will do so as one who is blind, and will die the death of ignorance. The Holy Prophet<sup>sa</sup>, in this Hadith, made no exception for any recipient of Divine revelation or a seer of true dreams. This clearly shows that if any recipient of revelation or one who experiences true dreams does not enter the fold of the Imam of the age, his end is most likely to be woeful, for it is clear that this Hadith is addressed to all believers and Muslims. Among them thousands have experienced dreams as well as Divine revelations in every age. In fact, among the followers of the Holy Prophet Muhammad[sa], there must have been tens of millions of persons who were blessed with Divine revelation. Bcsides, it is established by the Hadith and the Holy Quran that, at the time of the Imam of the age, if anyone has a true dream or receives a revelation, it would only be as a reflection of the light of the Imam of the age which falls upon willing hearts. The fact is that when the Imam of the age appears in the world, thousands upon thousands of lights accompany him and heaven is filled with joy. With the dissemination of spirituality and light, the right potentialities become alive. Anyone who has the capacity begins to experience a series of revelations. And anyone who has the capacity to pronounce judgement in matters of faith by the use of reason and reflection, his ability is enhanced. Anyone who has the inclination towards prayers is granted pleasure in his worship. Anyone who is engaged in debates with other faiths is given the power to argue and arrive at incontrovertible conclusions. All these blessings are in fact the outcome of the spiritual radiation which comes with the Imam of the age and descends upon the heart of every ready and eager person. This is a general law and a Divine practice to which we have been guided by the Holy Quran and authentic Hadith, and our personal experience have testified to it. The age of the Promised Messiah[as], however, has even greater distinction in that it is recorded in the books of earlier Prophets and Hadith of the Holy Prophet[sa] that, at the time of his advent, this radiation of spirituality will become so universal that women too will begin to receive revelations, minors will make prophecies, and ordinary people will be inspired by the Holy Spirit. All this will be a reflection of the spirituality of the Promised Messiah[as]. This is just like the light of the sun which falls upon a wall and illuminates it, and if the wall is white-washed with lime, it becomes all the more radiant. And if it is inlaid with mirrors, the light becomes too intense even for the eyes to behold. The wall, however, cannot claim this light as its own, for after sunset, not a trace of it remains. Likewise, all revelational light is a reflection of the light of the Imam of the age. Any right minded person—unless he is just unlucky, or is being tried and tested by God— will readily understand this fine point. If, God forbid, anyone fails to understand this Divine secret and, on hearing the news of the advent of the Imam of the age, does not establish communion with him, such a person initially shows indifference to the Imam, which then breeds estrangement, which in turn causes suspicions, and this produces hostility, which—God

forbid—ends up in the loss of faith. For instance,
when the Holy Prophet[sa] appeared, there were thousands of rabbis who were the recipient of revelations
and visions. They used to communicate the glad tidings that the advent of the Prophet of the Latter-days
was imminent. But when they did not accept the
Imam of the age who was *Khātamul Ambiyā*[10], they
were destroyed by the thunderbolt of Divine wrath,
and their ties with God Almighty were completely
severed. We need not mention everything about them
that has been recorded in the Holy Quran. These are
the people concerning whom the Holy Quran says:

$$\text{وَكَانُوْا مِنْ قَبْلُ يَسْتَفْتِحُوْنَ}^{11}$$

This verse means that these people did indeed invoke
Divine help for the success of faith and that they were
the recipient of revelations and visions. Even though
the Jews who had disobeyed Jesus[as] had fallen from
Divine grace, but they were absolved of this sin when
the Christian faith died on account of worshipping a human being and had lost its truth and spirituality. There
was then a rebirth of spirituality among them, and many of
them began to receive revelations and visions. There were
good and pious people among their rabbis. They used to

---

[10] The Seal of the Prophets[sa] **[Publishers]**
[11] *Al-Baqarah*, 2:90 **[Publishers]**

receive revelations to the effect that the Prophet of the Latter-days and the Imam of the time would appear soon. That is why certain godly scholars, after receiving revelation from God Almighty, immigrated to Arabia. Even their children knew that in the near future a new heavenly dispensation would be established. This is the significance of the verse:

$$\text{يَعْرِفُوْنَهٗ كَمَا يَعْرِفُوْنَ اَبْنَآءَهُمْ}^{12}$$

That is, they recognize this Prophet as clearly as they recognize their own children. But when that Promised Prophet[sa] did appear, self-conceit and prejudice doomed most of these rabbis, and their hearts turned black. Some fortunate ones, however, became Muslims and their Islam was indeed praiseworthy. This should lead us to fear God and to be very careful and cautious. Pray God, let no believer ever suffer the fate of Balaam. My Lord God! save this umma from all mischief, and safeguard it against the evil of Jews. Amen, repeat Amen.

Here it should be remembered that God Almighty has made tribes and nations with the object of setting up a physical system of civilization, so that, through mutual contact and relationship, cooperation and sympathy should prevail amongst mankind. In the

---

[12] *Al-Baqarah*, 2:147 [Publishers]

same way, He has established the system of Prophethood and Imāmat to establish spiritual relationship among the Holy Prophet's[sa] umma, and so that some should interceded for others.

Now, an important question arises: Who is to be called the Imam of the age? What are his hallmarks? And why is he to be preferred over other recipients of revelations, dreams and visions? The answer to this question is that the Imam of the age is the one for whose spiritual training God Almighty Himself assumes charge. He imbues his nature with such a light of Imāmat that he takes on all the rationalists and philosophers of the world, and vanquishes them in a comprehensive debate. Sustained as he is by God Almighty, he answers all subtle and abstruse questions in such an excellent manner, that one has to admit that he has come to this transient world equipped with all the provisions for its reform. As a result, he does not have to suffer embarrassment before an opponent. Spiritually speaking, he is the Commander-in-Chief of the forces of the Holy Prophet Muhammad[sa], and it is God Almighty's Will that through him faith should once again become victorious. All those who gather under his flag are also vouchsafed with capabilities of the highest order. He is blessed with all the necessary conditions essential to reform, and all the knowledge necessary for refuting objections, and for presenting the beauties of Islam. Furthermore, as God

Almighty knows that this Imam will have to confront the insolent and foul-mouthed people of the world He also gives him moral strength of the highest order. His heart is full of genuine compassion for mankind. But moral courage does not mean that he exercises clemency on every occasion without rhyme or reason, for it would be against moral wisdom. What it means is that these men are not like malicious and quick-tempered people who seethe with anger at every insult, and their faces betray the ugly signs of inner torture, also known as rage, and continue to rant and rave regardless of time and occasion. This is not the condition of those who are moral. True, they do sometimes use harsh words for the purpose of reform and in keeping with the demand of the occasion, but they do not get angry at heart, nor do they fly into a rage or froth at the mouth. Sometimes they do feign anger in order to overawe someone, while all the time their hearts are relaxed and happy and satisfied. That is why Jesus[as], on a number of occasions addressed others with harsh words, like 'swine', 'dogs', 'faithless', 'adulterous', etc., but we dare not say that he lacked the high moral qualities, for he himself taught these high morals and enjoined compassion. These words, which he frequently used, were not due to some fit of anger or frenzy, rather they were used with a calm and cool mind, and only on appropriate occasions. In short, it is essential for Imams to possess a perfect stan-

dard of moral excellence. A harsh word is not contrary
to moral condition if it is not the result of any bitterness
of temper and wild frenzy, and if it is appropriate and
necessitated by the occasion. It is worth mentioning that
the one whom God makes an Imam with His Own
hands, is also invested with the capabilities of Imāmat.
As mentioned in the verse:

$$ \text{اَعْطٰى كُلَّ شَىْءٍ خَلْقَهٗ} \text{ } ^{13} $$

Divine providence has equipped all animals and birds
with every faculty which, in the knowledge of God,
they would ever need. Similar is the case of those
whom God, in His eternal knowledge, wishes to en-
trust the task of Imāmat; they are given beforehand
many spiritual faculties that are necessary for Imāmat,
and the seed of all the capabilities that they might
need in the future is sown in their pure nature. As I
see it, an Imam must possess the following qualities
in order to benefit mankind.

**First** is moral strength. Since Imams come across
all sorts of miscreants and mean and foul-mouthed
people, it is essential for them to possess moral
strength of the highest order, so that they remain
immune against egoistic rage and wild frenzy and

---

[13] He gave unto everything its *proper* form.
—*Ṭā Hā*, 20:51 **[Publishers]**

people are not deprived of their blessings. It is shameful that a person called 'a friend of God' should fall prey to base morals, and should not even be able to tolerate a harsh word. Also, one who proclaims himself the 'Imam of the age', and yet has such a volatile temper that he starts frothing at the mouth and his eyes blaze with anger at the slightest provocation, can never be called an Imam of the age. The Imam of the age, therefore, must fully conform to the following verse:

$$ \text{اِنَّكَ لَعَلٰى خُلُقٍ عَظِيْمٍ} \ ^{14} $$

**Second** is the quality of Imāmat by virtue of which he is named the Imam. It means that he should have the eagerness to excel in good deeds, in acquiring Divine verities, and in his love and knowledge of God. This means that his soul should not be pleased at any deficiency nor be content with an imperfect state. He should be hurt if he is obstructed in his spiritual progress. This is the innate faculty that should be found in an Imam. Even if, perchance, people do not accept his teaching and enlightened guidance, or follow his spiritual light, he still remains the Imam by virtue of his innate spiritual strength. In short, this fine spiritual point is worth

---

[14] Thou dost surely possess high moral excellences.
—*Al-Qalam*, 68:5 **[Publishers]**

remembering that Imāmat is a faculty ingrained in the very nature of the person whom the Divine Will has designated for this office. The word 'Imāmat', when translated, means 'the power to lead'. Thus it is not a temporary office, which is given to him afterwards. In fact, like all the other faculties—of sight and sound and understanding—Imāmat is the faculty to forge ahead and to excel all in Divine matters. And this is what the term Imāmat implies.

**Third** faculty is the immensity of knowledge, which is sine qua non for Imāmat and its essential property. Since Imāmat implies the urge to move forward in truth and knowledge, in the essentials of love, and in sincerity and loyalty, an Imam focuses all his energies on this purpose, and always keeps praying [15]رَبِّ زِدْنِي عِلْمًا. His senses and perceptions are already equipped to perform these functions. That is why God's grace grants him all encompassing knowledge regarding Divine sciences and there is no one among his contemporaries who can equal him in the knowledge of Quranic verities, in spiritual blessings and in incontrovertible reasoning. His considered opinion corrects the opinion of others. Whenever someone disagrees

---

[15] O my Lord, increase me in knowledge.—*Tā Hā*, 20:115
**[Publishers]**

with him with regard to religious verities, the truth is always on his side. This is because the light of intuition helps him understand the true verities. No one else is granted this light with such brilliance.

$$ ذٰلِكَ فَضْلُ اللّٰهِ يُؤْتِيۡهِ مَنۡ يَّشَآءُ ^{16} $$

So just as a hen sits on its eggs and hatches young chicks, and transfers her qualities to them by keeping them under her feathers, so does the Imam, through his spiritual knowledge, mould his companions, and strengthens them in faith and in Divine knowledge. But such encompassing knowledge is not essential for other recipients of revelation and righteous people, because they are not entrusted with the training and education of mankind. It doesn't matter much if such pious people and seers suffer from a little ignorance and lack of knowledge; for they are not the captains of a ship, and are themselves in need of one. They should not utter such absurdities as to say, 'We do not stand in need of this spiritual captain, we are competent enough on our own.' They should remember that they do need him, just as a female needs a male. Hence, God has created everyone for a purpose. And anyone who claims to be an Imam while he has not

---

[16] That is Allah's grace; He bestows it on whom He pleases.— *Al-Jumuʿah*, 62:5 [Publishers]

been created for this purpose will only invite people's derision. He will be quite like a foolish mendicant who had invited ridicule in the presence of a king. The story goes that there lived a certain holy man in a city, who was righteous and God-fearing, but was quite ignorant. The king had faith in him, but his minister, who knew of his ignorance, did not. Once, when the king and his minister went to see him, the mendicant, dabbling in Islamic history, said to the king, 'Alexander of Rome, too has been a great king in this umma.' This provided the minister an opportunity to criticise. Promptly he submitted: 'Your Majesty, in addition to his spiritual expertise, the *Fakīr* is also a great scholar of history!'

Therefore, when confronting his opponents and ordinary seekers, the Imam of the age does not require revelation as much his intellectual ability, for there are all kinds of people who criticize the shariah on the basis of medicine, astronomy, physics, geography and authentic Islamic literature, as well as reason and textual knowledge. The Imam of the age is called the defender of the light of Islam. God Almighty pronounces him to be the gardener of this garden. He is obliged to refute every objection and silence every critic. Not only that, but also has to demonstrate to the world the beauty and excellence of Islam. Hence, such a person is worthy of great veneration and is a veritable philosopher's stone, for in his person Islam is revealed as a living religion. He is the pride of Islam and God's conclusive proof for all the people. No one has the right to forsake him, for by the Will and Pleasure of God, he is the defender of the honour of Islam, the well-wisher of all Muslims and encompasses the excellences of the faith like a circle. In every battle between Islam and unbelief, he alone is of real help. It is his holy breath that kills unbelief. He is the whole and the rest are his parts:

اوچوکل وتو چوجُزئی نے کلی        تو ہلاک استی گراز و ے بگسلی ¹⁷

The **Fourth** power is high resolve, which is essential for the Imam of the age. Resolve means not to get tired under any condition or to lose hope or to slacken in one's determination. Many a time, Prophets, Divine Messengers and *Muḥaddathīn*[18], who are the Imams of the age, are confronted with such trials and calamities, as if God Almighty has forsaken them and intends to destroy them. And many a time revelation and inspiration is suspended and they receive no revelation for a time. Many a time their prophecies appear

---

[17] Persian couplet:
*He is like the whole and you are just a part, not the whole;*
*You will perish if you break away from him.* [**Publishers**]
[18] Those who enjoy converse with God. [**Publishers**]

in the guise of trials and people at large do not understand their truth. Often the realization of their
objective is delayed for some time. And many a time,
they are like those who are forsaken, abandoned,
cursed and rejected. Everyone who hurls abuses at
them thinks that he is doing something laudable. Everyone despises them and looks down upon them with
disgust and doesn't even like to respond to their salutations. It is at such moments that their resolve is put
to the test. By no means do they lose their heart during such trials, nor do they relent in the performance
of their task until Divine succour arrives.

The **Fifth** power which is essential for the Imam of
the age is reliance upon God. This means that in times
of trial and tribulation, when they face a bitter enemy
and he demands a sign, or when they are in need of a
victory, and when it is imperative to help someone,
they incline towards God Almighty so much so that
their prayers, which are full of truth, sincerity, love,
faithfulness and unshakeable resolve, cause a commotion in heaven and their devoted and humble
supplications produce in heaven an uproar full of anguish, which creates a commotion among the angels.
Then, just as clouds begin to appear in the sky after a
very hot season, so does the warmth of their reliance
upon God, or the heat of their deep devotion to Him,
begin to shape something in the heavens. Destinies

change and Divine Will takes on different colours until the cool breezes of Providence begin to blow. And just as God creates the substance that causes fever, so does He create the antidote which expels it upon Divine command. Similar is the effect of the reliance which such people have upon God.

آں دُعائے شیخ نے چوں ہر دُعاست    فانی است و دستِ او دستِ خدا است [19]

And the trust which the Imam of the age places in God, i.e., his absorption in God, is more profound and effective than that of all the *Auliyā'*.[20] For instance, Moses[as] was the Imam of his age, and Balaam was the *Walī* of his time. He enjoyed communion with God and his prayers were accepted. When, however, Balaam confronted Moses[as], the contest destroyed Balaam, just as a sharp sword instantly severs the head from the body. The unfortunate Balaam, however, was unaware of the philosophy that, though God Almighty may speak to someone and declare him to be His beloved and elect, but when he confronts one who is more immersed in the waters of Divine grace, he will certainly be destroyed. Neither any revelation nor the fact that his prayers used

---

[19] Persian Couplet:
*That prayer of the Sheikh is no ordinary prayer;*
*He is mortal, yet his hand is the hand of God.* [Publishers]
[20] *Auliyā'*, plural of *Walī* (Saint). [Publishers]

to be accepted could save him. This was one Balaam, but thousands of such Balaams perished in the time of our Holy Prophet^sa, for most of the Jewish rabbis had become like Balaam after the demise of Christianity.

The **Sixth** requirement for the Imam is that he continues to receive visions and revelations one after the other. The Imam of the age often receives knowledge, truths and verities from God through revelation. The revelations of other people cannot be compared to these revelations, for both in quality and quantity they are far superior to those of other people. It is through them that [the gates of] knowledge are thrown open and Quranic truths are revealed and all the problems and difficulties relating to the faith are solved. Moreover, they manifest prophecies of the highest order that create an impact on the opponents. In short, visions and revelations of the Imams of the age are not merely confined to their persons but are extremely useful and auspicious in helping the faith, and strengthening the belief. God Almighty speaks to them very clearly and distinctly and answers their prayers. And many a time a dialogue ensues, whereby questions are followed by answers in quick succession. All this takes place in the form of such a pure, delectable and eloquent revelation that the recipient believes as if he were beholding God Himself. The revelation, the Imam of the age receives is not like the case of a person who surreptitiously throws a stone and runs away, without letting anyone know who he was and where he went. God Almighty, on the contrary, comes very close to them, slightly unveiling His Holy and Lustrous countenance which is all Light. This experience is not for others, who at times feel as if someone had been trifling with them. Revealed prophecies of the Imam of the age are tantamount to disclosing the unseen. In other words, they get a complete hold over the unseen, just as a rider has a horse under full control. The reason why their revelation is granted this vigour and [sense of] discovery, is that the pure revelations vouchsafed to them may not be mistaken for satanic inspirations, and may serve as incontrovertible arguments.

Let it be clearly understood that satanic inspirations are a fact, and ordinary seekers do receive them. Similarly, there is a self-suggestion known as confused dreams. Anyone who denies it, denies the Holy Quran, for it testifies to their existence. God Almighty says that as long as man's self is not fully cleansed and purified, it is possible for him to experience satanic inspirations, and he is described as:

عَلَى كُلِّ اَفَّاكٍ اَثِيمٍ ۝ [21]

---

[21] [They descend] on every great liar *and* sinner.
—*Al-Shuʿarāʾ*, 26: 223 **[Publishers]**

But the righteous are immediately informed about any satanic suggestion. Unfortunately, Christian clerics, while commenting on the incident whereby Jesus was tempted by the devil,[22] have dared to suggest that it was not something which actually happened, and which the world could see and the Jews could witness, but was rather a satanic inspiration which he received and rejected three times. One shivers to hear such an interpretation of the New Testament. Messiah[as] and satanic inspiration, indeed! Even if we don't believe this conversation to be a satanic inspiration, and imagine that Satan did really assume bodily form and met Jesus[as], the following objection would arise: If it were indeed true that Satan—the old serpent—really revealed himself in a corporeal form and took his stand near the sacred synagogue of the Jews, around which hundreds of people lived, then thousands of people must have gathered to see him. In fact Jesus[as] himself ought to have summoned the Jews and shown them the Satan whose very existence was denied by a number of their sects. And this in itself would be considered a sign for the Messiah[as], and many a people would have been rightly guided. Even the high-ranking officials of the Roman Empire would have

---

[22] Matthew, 4:8-9 **[Publishers]**

believed in Jesus when they beheld Satan and saw him flying. But nothing of the kind happened. This lends credence to the belief that this was a kind of spiritual conversation, which, in other words, can be called satanic inspiration. However, it reminds me that in Jewish literature many mischievous persons have been named Satan. In keeping with this usage, the Messiah[as] also gave the name of 'Satan'[23] to an honourable disciple of his, who was given the keys of heaven only a few verses before. So, it is also possible that some Jewish 'Satan' might have come to Jesus[as] to mock and ridicule him. And Jesus[as] might have called him 'Satan', just as he had called Peter, 'Satan'. The Jews were given to such mischief, and it is a peculiar characteristic of the Jews to pose such questions. Furthermore, it is also possible that this story is only a myth, recorded deliberately or mistakenly, for these gospels are not the gospels of the Messiah[as], nor have they ever been sanctified by him as such. On the contrary, they have been written by disciples or other people, according to their own perception and understanding. And this is why they differ from one another. We can, therefore, say that some of the writers could have been mistaken with

---

[23] Mathew, 16:23 **[Publishers]**

regard to this incident; just as some of the evangelists were mistaken in thinking that the Messiah[as] had died on the cross.[24] Such errors were ingrained in the very nature of the disciples, for the Gospels inform us that mentally they were not so perceptive. The Messiah[as] himself testifies that they were weak in intelligence, insight and ability. In any case, the fact is that no satanic thought can come to stay in the hearts of the pure. If any fleeting thought does ever come close to their hearts, it is immediately dispelled and put away and their clean slate remains spotless and clean. In the Holy Quran, such a doubt, which resembles a drab and half-baked thought, is called *Ṭā'if* طائف. In Arabic lexicon it is also known as *Ṭā'if* طائف, *Ṭauf* طوف, *Ṭay-yif* طيّف and *Ṭaif* طيف. A fleeting doubt of this kind has very little relationship with heart, in fact it has nothing at all to do with it. In fact such a doubt is like the faint shadow of a distant tree. And it is possible that the accursed Satan might have wanted to instil such a doubt in Jesus's[as] heart, and that Jesus[as], by his prophetic power, managed to dispel it. The reason why I have

---

[24] From among many Christian Gospels, one Gospel is still in their possession in which it is written that Jesus[as] did not die on the cross. This statement is correct, for *Marhami 'Īsa* [Jesus' Ointment], which has been mentioned by hundreds of physicians, bears it out. [**Author**]

had to mention all this is because this story does not only figure in the Gospels, but is also to be found in authentic Hadith. For instance, it is written:

عن محمد بن عمران الصيرفى قال حدثنا الحسن بن عليل العنزى عن العباس بن عبد الواحد عن محمد بن عمرو عن محمد بن مناذر عن سفيان بن عينه عن عمرو بن دينار عن طائوس عَنْ اَبِى هُرَيْرَةَ قَالَ جَاءَ الشَّيْطٰنُ اِلىٰ عِيْسىٰ قَالَ اَلَسْتَ تَزْعَمُ اَنَّكَ صَادِقٌ قَالَ بَلىٰ قَالَ فَاوِقْ عَلىٰ هذِهِ الشَّاهِقَةِ فَالْقِ نَفْسَكَ مِنْهَا فَقَالَ وَيْلُكَ اَلَمْ يَقُلِ اللّٰه يَا ابْنَ اٰدَمَ لَا تَبْلِنِى بِهَلَاكِكَ فَاِنِّىْ اَفْعَلُ مَااَشَاءُ

That is 'Muhammad bin Imran Sairfi reports from Hasan bin Aleel Anzi, and he from Abbas bin Abdul Wāhid, and he from Muhammad bin Amr, and he from Muhammad bin Manādhir, and he from Sufyan bin Aynah, and he from Amr bin Dinār, and he from Ṭaus, and he from Abu Huraira that Satan came to Jesus[as] and said: 'Dost thou not think that thou art truthful?' He said: 'Why not?' Satan said: 'If this is true, climb up this mountain, and throw yourself down.' Jesus[as] said: 'Woe to thee, dost thou not know that God has said: Do not try Me by thy own death, for I do what I will.'

It is obvious that Satan must have come to him, just as Gabriel comes to the Messengers. Gabriel does not come as people do, on a train or on a hired horse, wearing a turban and wrapped in a chador. Rather he

comes as if from the other world. Moreover, how can
Satan, who is so wretched, dare to come openly like a
man? In view of this discussion one can't help accepting the stand taken by Draper. But this much can be
said that Jesus[as] with his prophetic power and light of
truth never allowed any satanic inspiration to come
anywhere near him. Instead, he immediately set about
rejecting and repudiating it. And just as darkness cannot stand up against light, in the same way Satan could
not stand up against Jesus[as] and fled. This indeed is the
correct meaning of the verse:

$$ \text{اِنَّ عِبَادِیْ لَیْسَ لَکَ عَلَیْهِمْ سُلْطٰنٌ} \ ^{25} $$

Satan can only become dominant over those who suc-
cumb to his temptations and inspirations. But those
who strike Satan from a distance with the arrow of
light, and smite him in the face with the lash of rebuke,
and refuse to submit to any of his nonsense, are exempt from his sway. But since God Almighty wants
these people to see the kingdom of heaven and earth,
and Satan belongs to the kingdom of the earth, therefore, in order to attain full knowledge of the creation,
they must have a glimpse of the face of this bizarre
creature known as Satan and hear his speech. But this

---

[25] Surely, thou shalt have no power over My servants.—*Al-
Ḥijr*, 15:43 [Publishers]

does not in any way tarnish their purity and chastity. The Satan, in keeping with his age-old method of planting doubts, mischievously made a request to Jesus[as], which his pious nature spontaneously rejected and refused to accept. This did not in any way detract him from his lofty station. Do not villains sometimes speak in the presence of kings? It was thus, in spiritual terms, that Satan put his word into his heart. Jesus[as] did not accept this satanic inspiration and simply rejected it. This was indeed something praiseworthy. To criticise it is a folly and amounts to ignorance of spiritual philosophy. Not every saint or sufi can repel and expose the filth of satanic suggestion as Jesus[as] did with the whip of his light. Sayyid Abdul Qadir Jilani[ra][26] says, "I too received a satanic inspiration once. Satan said: 'O Abdul Qadir! all your prayers are accepted. From now on whatsoever is forbidden to others is lawful to you. You are even exempt from obligatory prayers. Do whatever you please.' At this, I said, 'Be off O Satan! how can something that was not permissible for the Holy Prophet[sa] be permissible for me!' After this, Satan disappeared from my sight along with his golden throne." Now, when even a man of God and a unique human like Abdul Qadir[ra] received a satanic inspira-

---

[26] Abdul Qadir Jilani: (d.1166) Sufi, saint and jurist.
**[Publishers]**

tion, how can ordinary humans, who have not yet fully accomplished their spiritual journey, be secure against it, for—unlike Sayyid Abdul Qadir[ra] and Jesus[as]—they lack the spiritual eyes with which to recognize satanic inspirations. Let it be remembered that the soothsayers who were found in large numbers in Arabia before the advent of the Holy Prophet[sa], frequently experienced satanic inspirations, on the basis of which they sometimes made prophecies. Curiously enough, some of their prophecies turned out to be true. Islamic literature is replete with such stories. Anyone, therefore, who denies satanic inspiration, denies all the teachings of the Prophets[as] as well as the very institution of Prophethood. It is recorded in the Bible that once four hundred prophets experienced a satanic inspiration and prophesied the victory of a king, having been fooled by a lying spirit.[27] But the king was killed in disgrace in the same battle, and his army suffered a great defeat. But there was one Prophet who had received a revelation through Gabriel, and had predicted beforehand that the king would be killed, dogs would eat his corpse and it would be a great defeat. This prophecy came to pass, but the prediction of four hundred prophets turned out to be wrong.

---

[27] 1Kings 22:6,23 [Publishers]

Now, when satanic inspirations are so frequent, one will naturally doubt the credibility of all revelations. No revelation would seem to be reliable in view of the possibility that it might be of satanic origin. More so, when the same thing happened to a great Prophet like Jesus$^{as}$. This seriously undermines the credibility of the recipients of revelation. Is revelation then a kind of ordeal? The answer to this question is that this is no occasion to lose heart, for it is the Divine Law that in this world everything valuable and precious is accompanied by adulterations. Look! there are pearls that are recovered from rivers and then there are cheap pearls which people make artificially and sell. Now the trade of genuine pearls cannot be stopped just because there are imitation pearls also, for the jewellers whom God Almighty has endowed with insight, recognize at a single glance the genuine pearl from the fake one. Hence, the jeweller of the pearls of revelation is the Imam of the age. By keeping his company, a person can readily distinguish between the real and the artificial. O mystics! O victims of this alchemy! tread this path with care and remember that true revelation, which is purely from God Almighty, is accompanied by the following signs:

1. It is experienced in a state when the fire of anguish melts a man's heart and it flows towards God Almighty like limpid water. This is what the Hadith refers to, which states that the Holy Quran was re-

vealed in a state of pathos, so you should recite it with a feeling of anguish.

2. True revelation is accompanied by a quality of pleasure and ecstasy; it bestows conviction for an unknown reason, and it penetrates the heart like a nail of steel and its wording is eloquent and free from error.

3. True revelation has a certain grandeur and loftiness about it; it hits the heart hard, and it descends upon it with might and with an awesome voice. On the contrary, false revelation is marked by a faint voice like that of thieves, eunuchs and females, for Satan is a thief, a eunuch and a woman.

4. True revelation carries in it the effect of Divine powers. And it is essential that it should contain prophecies that come to be fulfilled.

5. True revelation continues to make a person more and more pious with each passing day, and cleanses his inner impurities and filth, and enhances his moral condition.

6. True revelation is testified by all the inner faculties of a man, which are illumined by a new and divine light. He finds a change in himself, his earlier life suffers death and a new life begins, and he becomes a medium of compassion for mankind at large.

7. True revelation does not end with a single revelation, for God's voice has continuity. He is most Kind.

He speaks to whosoever He blesses with His attention, and answers his questions. His supplications are answered at the same place and in the same instant, though at times there comes a break.

8. The recipient of true revelation is never a coward and is not afraid to confront an opponent who himself claims to receive revelations, no matter how hostile he may be. He knows that God is with him and that He will cause his opponent to suffer a disgraceful defeat.

9. True revelation is a means for understanding spiritual verities and sciences, for God does not wish to keep the recipient of His revelation ignorant and devoid of knowledge.

10. True revelation is also accompanied by many other blessings. One who has converse with God is granted honour and awe inspiring prestige by heaven.

The present age is so flawed that most of the philosophically disposed persons, naturalists[28], and the followers of Brahmu faith[29] deny revelation of this kind. Many have departed from this world in this state

---

[28] Naturalists refer to those who believe that all religious truth is derived from nature and natural causes, and not from revelation. [Publishers]
[29] Brahmu Samāj (literally 'Divine Society') a Hindu sect founded in 1828. [Publishers]

of denial. But the truth remains the truth, even if the entire world denies it, and falsehood remains falsehood, even though the whole world endorses it. Those who believe in the existence of God Almighty and consider Him to be the Architect of the universe, and know Him to be the All-Seeing, the All-Hearing and the All-Knowing, would be foolish not to believe that He speaks as well. Can He not speak Who sees and knows, and Whose knowledge encompasses each and every minuscule particle without the aid of any physical means? And, it is also wrong to say that though His attribute of speech was functioning in the past, it no longer does so, as if to say, that His attribute of speech is a thing of the past and is no more. Such a belief produces hopelessness. If some of God's attributes do in fact become redundant after a time, and not even a trace of them is left, then all His other attributes also become doubtful. Woe betides such minds and such beliefs! After accepting all the attributes of God Almighty, they get hold of a knife and excise a vital part of these attributes and throw it away. It is a pity that Āryas put a seal on Divine revelation after the Vedas, and the Christians did likewise, as if mankind needed eye-witnessed revelation for their personal enlightenment and spiritual knowledge, only until the time of Jesus[as], and future generations are so unfortunate as to have been deprived of it permanently. While the fact is that man is ever in need of direct experience and personal insight. A religion can only survive as living knowledge as long as God Almighty's attributes continue to manifest themselves afresh; otherwise it becomes mere tales and soon dies out. Can human conscience accept such failure? How can God Almighty's grace shut the door of revelation upon us, when we find ourselves in need of such absolute knowledge as is not possible without converse with God and without great heavenly signs? Have our hearts in these times changed or has God become a different God? We do admit that the revelation vouchsafed to one man at one time can refresh the spiritual knowledge of millions, and that it is not necessary for each and every person to receive it, but we can never admit that revelation should be completely done away with and we should be left with mere tales which none of us has witnessed. It is quite evident that when a matter continues to remain in the form of a story for hundreds of years and there is no fresh example for its verification, most philosophically-minded persons will not accept such tales without strong evidence, particularly when such tales relate to phenomena which are considered contrary to reason in this age. That is why, with the passage of time, people with the philosophical bent of mind have been ridiculing such miracles, and they do not give them any credence at all. In this, they are quite justified because they feel in their heart of hearts that if God is unchanged, and His attributes are unchanged, and our need is also the same as before, and every soul is crying out for spiritual enlightenment, then why should revelation have ceased? Millions of Hindus have turned atheists, for the pundits have repeatedly taught them that revelation has been at an end for millions of years. Their hearts were thus assailed by the thought that if revelation is indeed a fact, why should it have ceased after the Vedas, while they are in greater need of fresh revelations from Parmeshwar.[30]

That is why atheism has become rampant in the land of Āryas, and this is why you will find hundreds of sects among the Hindus that mock at the Vedas and reject them. One of these are the Jains, and also the Sikhs who parted with Hinduism for similar reasons. This is because, in Hinduism, hundreds of objects have been considered partners with God. There is such a plethora of polytheistic beliefs that it is hard to find any trace of Parmeshwar. Likewise, the Divine origin of the Vedas is a claim based only on a baseless myth going back millions of years, and it is not substantiated by any fresh evidence. That is why the orthodox Sikhs

---

[30] Supreme Being in Hindu religion. [Publishers]

do not believe in the Vedas. In this connection a Sikh gentleman has written an article which appeared in *Akhbār-e-'Ām,* 26th September, 1898, in which he quotes verses from the *Granth* to prove that the Khalsas do not believe in the Vedas, and this is what the Gurus have taught. True, the writer does not profess allegiance to the Holy Quran either. This is because the Sikhs have no knowledge of Islam and are unaware of the light which God Almighty has invested it with. Nor, because of ignorance and prejudice, have they any knowledge of the light which the Holy Quran is suffused with. And, as a community, they are related more closely to the Hindus than the Muslims. Otherwise it should have been enough for them if they had followed the testament which Baba Nanak Sahib has left inscribed on his *Chola Sahib*[31], viz., there is no true religion except Islam. It is indeed a great pity to disregard such an important testament of such a holy person, for *Chola Sahib* is the only personal relic of Baba Sahib left with the Khalsas. As for the verses of *Granth Sahib,* they were collected much later, and researchers have quite a few reservations about them. God alone knows how many interpolations have crept therein and how many people have contributed to this

---

[31] Cloak worn by Baba Nanak, on which verses of the Holy Quran are inscribed. **[Publishers]**

collection. Anyhow, this is not what we are discussing, for our aim is to point out that, for the purpose of keeping the faith of mankind ever fresh, there is always the need for fresh revelation. Such revelations are recognized by their authority, for no devil, demon or evil spirit has this authority, except God. The revelation vouchsafed to the Imam of the age gives credence to other revelations.

We have already stated that the Imam of the age has in his nature the innate power of Imāmat, and Providence invests him with the quality of leadership. It is the way of God that He does not like to see mankind divided and dispersed. Just as He has included a number of planets in the solar system, and has given the sun sovereignty over them, so does He invest the ordinary believers with light in keeping with their spiritual station, and appoints the Imam of the age as their Sun. This Divine practice exists in His creation to such an extent that it is found even among the honeybees. They too have an Imam—known as [32]يعسوب. In worldly kingdoms also God Almighty has so willed that a nation should have a leader or a king. May God's curse be on those who like dissention and do not obey the Amīr, despite the Divine command:

---

[32] *Ya'sūb*: The queen bee. **[Publishers]**

أَطِيْعُوااللّٰهَ وَأَطِيْعُواالرَّسُوْلَ وَأُولِي الْأَمْرِ مِنْكُمْ ³³

In worldly terms, *Ūlul Amr* means the king, and in spiritual terms it means the Imam of the age. Since anyone who is not against our objectives and is physically useful to our faith, is one of us, that is why, my advice to the Jamāʿat is that they should consider British rule as *Ūlul Amr* and should obey them sincerely, for they do not interfere with our religious affairs. Rather we feel secure on account of their presence. And it will be dishonest on our part, not to acknowledge the British who have helped our faith in a way which even some Muslim rulers of Hindustan failed to provide. Some of these rulers, in their cowardliness, had abandoned the province of the Punjab. As a result, we and our religion suffered great hardship at the hands of various Sikh rulers. So much so that even offering congregational prayers in the mosques and proclaiming *Adhān* had become difficult. Islam, as a religion, was as good as dead in Punjab. Then came the British, and with them our good fortune also returned. They helped Islam and granted us full freedom in the performance of our religious obligations; our mosques were redeemed to us, and, after a long time,

---

³³ Obey Allah, and obey *His* Messenger and those who are in authority over you — *Al-Nisāʾ*, 4:60 [Publishers]

Islam once again began to be openly practised in the
Punjab. Is such kindness not worthy of being remembered? The fact is that some of the spine-less Muslim
rulers had, on account of their negligence, pushed us
into the land of disbelief, but the British, catching hold
of our hands and saved us. To indulge in seditious in-
trigues against the British, therefore, amounts to
forgetting the blessings of God Almighty.

Reverting to the original topic, I would like to say
that just as the Holy Quran requires of us that we
should submit to the one ruler in our physical life, it
expects the same from us in our spiritual life. It is in
this context that God Almighty teaches us the prayer:

$$ اِهْدِنَا الصِّرَاطَ الْمُسْتَقِيْمَ ۞ $$

$$ صِرَاطَ الَّذِيْنَ اَنْعَمْتَ عَلَيْهِمْ ۚ ^{34} $$

One should reflect, therefore, that no believer—in
fact, no man or even animal—is deprived of Divine
favours, yet we cannot say that God Almighty com-
mands us to follow them all. This verse, therefore,
means that we beseech God to grant us the good fortune of following the path of those who were the
recipients of the downpour of spiritual favours in a

---

[34] Guide us in the right path, the path of those on whom Thou
hast bestowed *Thy* blessings.—*Al-Fātiḥah*, 1:6-7 **[Publishers]**

perfect and consummate way. So this verse actually tells us that we should be with the Imam of the age.

Let it be remembered that the term 'Imam of the age' comprises all Prophets, Messengers, *Muḥaddath-īn* and *Mujaddadīn*. But those who are not appointed by God to educate and guide God's creatures, nor have they been vouchsafed such excellences, regardless of their being saints or seers, cannot be called the Imams of the age.

Finally we come to the question: Who is the Imam in the present age, whom all Muslims, all righteous people, and all those who experience true dreams or revelations must follow. I hereby proclaim, without any hesitation, that, by the grace and bounty of God,

### I am the Imam of the age.

He has brought together in my person all these signs and conditions and sent me at the turn of this century, of which fifteen years have already passed. I appeared at a time when all Islamic teachings, without any exception, were riddled with differences. Likewise, in respect of the Messiah's[as] descent, extremely false notions had gained currency. Differences were so great that some believed Jesus[as] to be alive while others believed him to be dead; some believed in his bodily descent, while others believed in metaphorical descent. Some thought he would descend in Damascus, others in Mecca, and still others in Jerusalem. Some expected him to appear in the army of Muslims, and some thought he would descend in India. All these differing beliefs and statements called for a *Ḥakam* [Arbitrator] to come and judge between them. And I am that *Ḥakam*. I have been sent to break the Cross, in the spiritual sense, and to remove these differences. These were the two reasons that necessitated my advent. Although it was not necessary for me to produce any other evidence in support of my truthfulness—for necessity is evidence enough—even then God Almighty has manifested numerous signs in my support. Therefore, just as I am the *Ḥakam* to pronounce judgement in all the other differences, so am I the *Ḥakam* in the dispute over the life and death of Jesus[as]. I declare that the stand taken by Imam Malik[rh35], Ibn Hazm[rh36] and the Muʻtazilites[37], with regard to the death of the Messiah[as], is correct, and I believe the rest of the Ahl-i-Sunnah to be in the wrong. Therefore, in my capacity as *Ḥakam,* I

---

[35] Imam of Jurisprudence. Compiler of *Al-Muʼaṭṭā* (716-795 AD). **[Publishers]**

[36] Andalusian jurist, theologian, author. (994-1064). **[Publishers]**

[37] An Early Islamic school of thought. (800-900). **[Publishers]**

hereby give the verdict that the Ahl-i-Sunnah are right only as far as the basic concept of Jesus' descent is concerned, for he was bound to descend, albeit in the spiritual sense. Where they have erred, is in the manner of descent, for it was to be figurative, not literal. On the question of the death of Jesus[as], the Mu'tazilites, Imam Malik, Ibn Hazm, and others who hold similar views, are in the right, for according to the clear authority of the blessed verse[38] فَلَمَّاتَوَفَّيْتَنِىْ the Messiah[as] must have died before the Christians had gone astray. This is my verdict as the *Ḥakam*. He who does not accept it, does not accept Him Who has sent me as the *Ḥakam*. If the question is asked, 'What is the proof of your being the *Ḥakam*?' The answer is that the time for which the *Ḥakam* was destined is here, and so are the people whose wrong notions about the Cross the *Ḥakam* was meant to rectify. The signs which were to appear in support of the *Ḥakam* have appeared, and they continue to appear. The heaven is manifesting the signs and so is the earth. Blessed be those whose eyes are not closed.

I do not ask you just to believe in the signs that have already appeared, rather I ask you to challenge

---

[38] But since Thou didst cause me to die.—*Al-Mā'idah*, 5:118
[Publishers]

my signs if you do not think that I am the *Ḥakam*. It is useless to argue against me, for I have come at the time of the divergence of creeds. Only the debate about the [person of] *Ḥakam* is open to all, and I have elaborated upon it. God has given me four signs:

1. I have been given the sign of eloquence and mastery in Arabic, as a reflection of the Quranic miracle of eloquence, and no one can challenge me on this.

2. I have been given the sign of expressing the truths and verities of the Holy Quran, and no one can challenge me on this.

3. I have been given plentiful signs of the acceptance of prayers, and no one can challenge me on this. I can affirm on oath that nearly thirty thousand of my prayers have been accepted, and of which I have proof.

4. I have been vouchsafed the sign of the knowledge of the unseen, and no one can challenge me on this.

These are the Divine testimonies granted to me. Likewise, the prophecies of the Holy Prophet[sa] about me have been fulfilled like manifest signs.

آسماں بار دنشان الوقت سے گویدز میں   ایں دوشاہداز بے تصدیق من استادہ اند [39]

---

[39] Persian couplet:
*The heavens rain signs, the earth says: now is the time;*
*These two witnesses stand ready to testify for me.* [Publishers]

It has now been a long time since the solar and lunar eclipses occurred during the month of Ramadan. I have also been barred from the Hajj. The plague, in accordance with the Hadith, has spread in the land. Countless signs have been shown through me, which have been witnessed by thousands of Hindus and Muslims, and I have not mentioned here. In view of all this, I am the Imam of the age, and God's support is with me. He guards me with a sharp sword. Also, I have been informed that whoever mischievously stands up against me, will be disgraced and put to shame. Look! I have communicated the injunction with which I was entrusted. I have frequently written about these issues in my books, but the incident that has induced me to return to them once again, is an error of judgement by a friend of mine, having learnt of which I wrote this booklet with a great anguish in my heart.

The details of this episode are as follows: In September, 1898 A.D., which conforms to *Jamādi-ul-Awwal,* 1316 A.H., a friend of mine—whom I believed to be innocent, devout and God-fearing, and of whom I have always thought well [40](وَاللّٰهُ حَسِيْبُهُ) but whom I now believe to be mistaken in some of his thinking, and I remain anxious lest it should cause

---

[40] God is the One to judge him. [Publishers]

him any harm—travelled to Qadian with a respected
friend of mine to see me. He recounted before me a
number of revelations he said he had received. I was
very much pleased to know that God Almighty had
honoured him with revelations. However, in the
course of narrating his revelations, he related to me a
dream in which he had said with regard to me, 'Why
should I pledge *Bai'at* at his hand, it is he who
should pledge allegiance to me!' From this I learnt
that he did not believe me to be the Promised Messiah, and that he was unaware of the true concept of
Imāmat. Therefore, sympathy on my part demanded
that I should write this booklet in order to explain to
him the doctrine of true Imāmat and to spell out the
importance of *Bai'at*. I have already written at length
about the true Imam who is entitled to accept *Bai'at*,
now I will say something about the true concept of
*Bai'at*. The term *Bai'at* is derived from *Bai'*, which
means a transaction carried out by mutual agreement,
in which something is bartered for another. The sine
qua non of *Bai'at* is that one who enters into it, sells
his being, with all its wherewithal, at the hands of a
spiritual guide, in order to acquire in exchange the
knowledge of spiritual verities and perfect blessings
which lead to Divine knowledge, salvation and favour of the Almighty. This shows that repentance is
not the sole object of *Bai'at*, for a person can have

recourse to it on his own. The true object of *Bai'at* is
to acquire the spiritual knowledge, blessings and
signs which brings about true repentance. The real
purpose of *Bai'at* is to enslave oneself to the spiritual leader and guide, and to acquire, in exchange,
the knowledge, spiritual insight and blessings which
help to fortify the faith and sharpen the spiritual vision and establish a pure relationship with God.
Likewise, it offers salvation from the hell of this
world and, consequently, of the hereafter. And, having cured the blindness of this world, it makes one
immune from the blindness of the hereafter. In the
presence of such a man who offers these fruits of
*Bai'at*, it would be the height of misfortune to turn
away from him knowingly. My dear friend! as for
ourselves, we are hungry and thirsty for spiritual
knowledge, for truths and verities and for heavenly
blessings, and even an ocean of knowledge is not
enough to satisfy us. If, therefore, anyone seeks to
have me as his follower, he can easily do so by way
of this transaction, keeping in mind the significance
and true philosophy of *Bai'at*. If he has such truths
and verities to offer as have not been vouchsafed to
me, or if some Quranic profundities have been disclosed to him which have not been disclosed to me,
then such a holy man is welcome to take my allegiance, and to give me in return those spiritual

verities, Quranic truths and heavenly blessings. I do
not wish to inconvenience him. If my inspired friend
can only expound in public the truths and verities of
surah *Al-Ikhlās*, and if I fail, on my part, to expound
its verities which are a thousand times superior to
his, then I shall submit myself before him.

ندارد کسے با تو ناگفتہ کار    ولیکن چو گفتی دلیلش بیار ⁴¹

In any case, if you possess the truths, the spiritual
verities and the blessings, that are miraculous in nature, then not only myself, but all my followers will
also enter into your *Bai'at*. Only an extremely unfortunate person will refuse to do so. I do not know how
to put it, but I am sorry to have to mention that when I
heard your revelations, I noticed in them a number of
grammatical errors. Pray, do not take offence; it is
only out of honest intent, humility and religious obli-
gation that I mention this. But, at the same time, I do
not believe that grammatical error in a revelation received by an ignorant or illiterate person, makes that
revelation in any way objectionable. This is a very
profound and delicate issue which requires detailed
consideration, but this is not the occasion for it. A

---

[41] Persian couplet:
*If you have nothing to say, nobody will bother you;*
*But since you have spoken, bring forth your arguments.*
**[Publishers]**

sanctimonious mullah—being unaware of the spiritual philosophy—may be excused if he flies into a rage on coming across such errors. But such revelations are of a much lower order, and are not illumined by the full blaze of Divine light, for revelation is of three kinds: low, middling and high.

In any case, I felt embarrassed at these errors and I prayed in my heart that my honoured friend may not mention these revelations, which are seemingly objectionable, before a mischievous and dry-brained mullah, for he might make fun of him. A revelation, which is devoid of truth or spiritual verities and is so full of errors, cannot be of any benefit to a friend or foe, particularly in this age. It is more likely to do him harm than good. I swear on my faith that what I say is nothing but the truth. My dear friend,[42] focus your attention more and more on God, for as the purity of the heart increases, so will the revealed word becomes more and more eloquent. The reason why the Quranic revelation is superior to the revelations of all other Prophets—both with regard to its verities and its eloquence—is that our Holy Prophet[sa] was granted greater purity of heart than anyone else. Thus with re-

---

[42] I am sure if this respected gentleman pays greater attention, his revelations may soon assume a kind of perfection. [**Author**]

spect to its content this revelation took the form of
spiritual verities, and in respect of its diction it took
the form of eloquence. My friend should also remember that *Bai'at*, as I have explained before, is a
transaction. I do not believe that even a thousandth
part of the truths and profundities of the Holy Quran
which distinguish the sermons of my learned friend,
Maulawī Abdul Karim Sahib, can be expressed by
this gentleman. The reason is that his revelational experience is still defective, and so is his learning. I am
not sure if he has ever had the occasion to study the
Holy Quran from a scholar.[43]

For God's sake, do not be offended. You have not
yet understood the significance of *Bai'at*, and you do
not realize what you have to surrender and what you
get in return. In our Jamā'at and among those servants of God Almighty who have pledged *Bai'at*

---

[43] Note:—I do not deny that springs of spiritual knowledge
could open to you. This, however, is not the case yet. Dreams
and visions are subject to figurative and metaphysical interpretation but you took your dream literally. The *Mujaddid* of
Sirhind saw in a vision that the Holy Prophet[sa] was granted the
rank of *Khalīlullāh* through him. And what is more Shah Wal-
iullah Sahib saw in a vision as though the Holy Prophet[sa] had
pledged *Bai'at* at his hand. But because of the depth of his
knowledge he did not think the way you did, and interpreted
the vision.[**Author**]

with me, there is a profound scholar of great excellence, by the name of Maulawī Ḥakīm Ḥāfiẓ Al-Ḥāj Nūr-ud-Dīn Sahib^ra. Just as he possesses a collection of virtually all the commentaries of the Holy Quran, so is his heart a virtual storehouse of thousands of Quranic verities. If you have indeed been given the privilege to receive *Bai'at*, then do try and teach Maulawī Sahib the truths and verities contained in just one part of the Holy Quran. Were these people insane to have entered into *Bai'at* at my hand, and to have rejected all other recipients of revelation? It would have been better for you if you had followed the example of Ḥaḍrat Maulawī Sahib^ra. Just reflect, is it for nothing that he has left his home and hearth and has come to me, and is living in a mud-house in great inconvenience? My worthy and dear friend— the recipient of revelation—had better remember that he is seriously mistaken if he thinks so. First of all if, by his spiritual power, he demonstrates before Ḥaḍrat Maulawī Sahib^ra a specimen of his own Quranic scholarship and, with its supernatural light, is able to receive *Bai'at* from such a lover of the Holy Quran as Nūr-ud-Dīn^ra, then I and all my Jamā'at will be at his service. Is it possible for a person, merely with the help of a few dubious and mostly incorrect words of revelation, to consider himself the Imam of the age? My dear friend! there are many prerequisites for the Imam of the age, and it is because of them that he is able to challenge the whole world.

ہزارنکتہ باریک تر زمُواینجاست    نہ ہرکہ سر بتراشد قلندری داند [44]

My dear 'claimant to revelation' should not be deceived by the fact that he often receives words by way of revelation. The truth is that there are many such people among my followers, and the revelations of some of them would constitute a whole book. Sayyid Amir Ali Shah, for instance, sends me a whole page of revelations every week. There are also women who bear witness to my claim and receive revelations in Arabic, without having learned a word of Arabic. Surprisingly enough, her[45] revelations contain far fewer errors than yours. On 28th September, 1898, I received a few of her revelations in a letter through her real brother Fateh Muhammad Buzdar. Many other followers of mine are also recipients of revelation. One of them resides in Lahore. But can such revelations release anyone from the necessity of pledging allegiance to the

---

[44] Persian couplet:
*Herein lie a thousand points, finer than hair;*
*Not everyone who gets his head shaved knows Qalandarī (renunciation).* [Publishers]
[45] Ghulam Fatima, daughter of Muhammad Khan Buzdar of Leiah. [Publishers]

Imam of the age? I do not mind pledging *Bai'at* to anyone, but the object of *Bai'at* is to acquire spiritual knowledge and to fortify one's faith. Tell me, then, what spiritual knowledge would you teach to those who pledge *Bai'at* to you, and what verities of the Holy Quran will you disclose to them? Please come and demonstrate the wonders of your Imāmat, and we will gladly pledge *Bai'at* at your hand.

حضرت ناصح گرآئیں دیدہ ودل فرش راہ     پر کوئی مجھ کو تو سمجھائے کہ سمجھائینگے کیا <sup>46</sup>

I proclaim to one and all that whatever God has bestowed upon me serves as a sign of my Imāmat. I am ready to surrender myself in *Bai'at* to anyone who exhibits these signs of Imāmat, and proves that he surpasses me in these qualities. But God's promises are immutable. No one can defy Him. Some twenty years ago the following revelation was recorded in *Brāhīn-e-Ahmadiyya*.

اَلرَّحْمٰنُ عَلَّمَ الْقُرْآنَ ۔ لِتُنْذِرَ قَوْمًا مَا اُنْذِرَ آبَاؤُ هُمْ وَلِتَسْتَبِيْنَ سَبِيْلُ الْمُجْرِمِيْنَ قُلْ اِنِّىْ اُمِرْتُ وَ اَنَا اَوَّلُ الْمُؤْمِنِيْنَ <sup>47</sup>

---

<sup>46</sup> *The revered admonisher is welcome—I am all eyes and ears for him;*
*But pray someone tell me what advice he will dole out!*
                                                    **[Publishers]**
<sup>47</sup> The most Gracious One has taught thee the Quran so that thou mightst warn a people whose ancestors have not been

According to this revelation, God has vouchsafed to me the knowledge of the Quran and has named me *Awwal-ul-Muminīn* [the first of the believers]. He has filled me with spiritual verities and truths like an ocean. He has revealed to me again and again that no one can equal me in my love for God and His recognition. God is my witness that I am ready for this contest. He who does not accept me will regret it after death, for he is under the Divine argument.

My dear, nothing whether related to the world or to the faith, can be adequately performed without competence. I remember that once a young man of a noble house—who was an absolute ignoramus and did not even know Urdu—appeared before a British official [with recommendation] to be appointed a Tehsildar. The British official said, 'Who will decide the cases for him if I make him a Tehsildar? I can't give him any post worth more than five rupees.' In the same way, God also says:

اَللّٰهُ اَعۡلَمُ حَيۡثُ يَجۡعَلُ رِسَالَتَهٗ ۘ [48]

Is it worthy of a person to whom thousands of friends and foes bring their questions and objections, and who is ap-

---

warned and so that the way of the guilty ones might become manifest. Tell them: I have been commissioned and I am the first of the believers. [Publishers]

[48] Allah knows best where to place His Message—*Al-An'ām*, 6:125 [Publishers]

pointed to represent Prophethood, that he should have just a few revealed sentences to his credit, and those too without any proof? Can this be enough to satisfy his people and his opponents?

I now wish to close this discussion. If there be anything unpalatable in it, I apologize to everyone, as I do also to my friend who claims to be the recipient of revelations. I have written all this in sheer good faith. I love this dear friend of mine with all my heart, and beseech God to be with him.

The humble one,
Mirza Ghulam Ahmad,
Qadian,
Distt. Gurdaspur.

# Maulawī Abdul Karim's Letter to a Friend[49]

بِسْمِ اللّٰهِ الرَّحْمٰنِ الرَّحِيْمِ　　اَلْحَمْدُ لِوَلِيِّهٖ وَالصَّلٰوةُ وَالسَّلَامُ عَلٰى نَبِيِّهٖ [50]

From Abdul Karim,
To my brother and dear friend Nasrullah Khan,

سَلَامٌ عَلَيْكُمْ وَرَحْمَةُ اللّٰهِ وَبَرَكَاتُهٗ [51]

Today, I again feel the need to relate to you the story of my aching heart, with the hope that you will share my feelings. But this need is not without a motive, for the Mover of hearts does not encourage His servants to do anything without purpose.

Chaudhry Sahib! I too am a son of Adam and born of a weak woman, and I too have to overcome human weaknesses, attractions of my loved ones, and other inadequacies. A person born of a woman cannot be hard hearted unless circumstances make him so. My

---

[49] It was only by chance that I happened to come across this letter, which brother Maulawī Abdul Karim Sahib has written to his friend. Since it has to do with the subject of this booklet I have published it here. **[Author]**

[50] In the name of Allah, the Gracious, the Merciful. Praise be to His Friend and peace and blessings upon His Prophet[sa].

**[Publishers]**

[51] Peace be on you and mercy of Allah and His blessings.

**[Publishers]**

old mother, who is soft-hearted and chronically ill, is still alive, and so is my father. [52] اَللّٰهُمَّ عَافِهٖ وَ وَالِهٖ وَ وَفِّقْهُ لِلْحُسْنٰى I have brothers who are so near and dear to me, and I have other relations as well. Do you think I have a heart of stone that I have been staying here for months on end. Or have I taken leave of my senses? Or do I blindly follow something and am I utterly ignorant of spiritual knowledge? Or am I known in my family, neighbourhood or town as a man who leads a life of sin? Or am I a pauper who keeps changing his guises to satisfy his hunger? [53] يَعْلَمُ اللّٰهُ وَ الْمَلَائِكَةُ يَشْهَدُوْنَ I am, by the grace of God, free from all such shortcomings.

ولا ازکی نفسی ولکن اللہ یزکی من یشاء [54]

Then what is it that has produced in me such steadfastness that has overcome all my other relationships? It is easily explained in one word: it is the recognition of the Imam of the age. And it is such a wonderful thing that it breaks up all other bonds and chains. You are well aware that to the best of my ability, I am familiar with the spiritual verities and inner meanings of the Book of God. At home, I have no occupation other than reading and teaching the Holy

---

[52] May God protect him, and be his Friend, and may goodness be his lot. **[Publishers]**

[53] God knows and the angels bear witness. **[Publishers]**

[54] Arabic phrase: I do not hold my self pure, but God purifies whomsoever He pleases. **[Publishers]**

Book. What then do I learn here? Is it not enough for the satisfaction of my soul that I should study at home and be acclaimed by so many people? No, by God, never! I used to study and teach the Holy Quran and on Fridays I used to occupy the pulpit and delivered moving moral sermons, warning the congregation against Divine chastisement and admonishing them to keep away from sin, but my inner self would always reproach me:

$$\text{لِمَ تَقُوْلُوْنَ مَا لَا تَفْعَلُوْنَ ۝}$$

$$^{55}\text{كَبُرَ مَقْتًا عِنْدَ اللهِ اَنْ تَقُوْلُوْا مَا لَا تَفْعَلُوْنَ ۝}$$

I moved others to tears, but did not weep myself. I dissuaded others from improper words and deeds, but never desisted from them myself. Since I was neither a hypocrite nor a selfish cheat, and the acquisition of fame and wealth was never my objective, these ideas crowded my mind whenever I had a moment to myself. But since I couldn't see any way of reforming myself, and my faith wouldn't let me be satisfied with such false rituals, I succumbed under these pressures and became seriously ill with heart-disease. Many a time I resolved to give up studying, teaching and preaching, but would eagerly return to devour books on ethics,

---

[55] Why do you say what you do not do? Most hateful is it in the sight of Allah that you say what you do not do.—*Al-Ṣaff*, 61:3-4 **[Publishers]**

mysticism and exegeses of the Holy Quran. With the same object I closely studied *Iḥyā'ul 'Ulūm, 'Awāriful M'ārif, Fatūḥāti Makkiya* all four volumes, as well as a large number of other books. As for the Holy Quran, it was the delight of my heart and, thank God, it still is. From childhood, indeed since infancy, my fondness for this holy and great scripture is too deep to describe in words. As my knowledge became more extensive, I acquired the skill to gratify audiences and embellish my sermons with many fine and amusing anecdotes. I even found that many sick people got cured at my hands. And yet there was no change in my own self. At last, after a great deal of hesitation and suspense, it was disclosed to me that this dirt would not wash off, unless I met a living exemplar or arrived at the fountain of life which alone could cleanse all inner impurities. Just look at how, for 23 years, the Perfect Guide and the Seal of Prophets[sa] led his Companions through the stages of spiritual evolution. The Holy Quran was the knowledge and the Holy Prophet[sa] was its true personification. It was not merely the grandeur and majesty of the eloquence of the Holy Quran, or its erudite style, that overawed the hearts in such an extraordinary manner. Rather, it was the practical example of the Holy Prophet[sa], his unique moral qualities, accompanied by the constant manifestation of heavenly signs, that made an indelible impression on the hearts of his

Companions. Since Islam was very dear to God
Almighty and He wanted it to live to the end of time,
He did not wish that it should become, like the other
faiths, a relic of outdated legends and myths. In every
age this blessed religion has had living exemplars who,
by their enlightened knowledge and example, made people remember the time of the Holy Prophet<sup>sa</sup>, to whom
the Holy Quran was revealed. In our own time, and in
keeping with this His practice, God Almighty has raised
the Promised Messiah<sup>as</sup> among us, so that he should be a
witness to the age. I had intended to state in this letter a
few intuitional arguments to underline the need for the
True Imam. But, only the day before yesterday, the
Promised Messiah<sup>as</sup> has himself completed a book, in the
context of certain exigencies, which relates to the necessity for an Imam, and it is to be published shortly. I have,
therefore, dropped my own idea in this regard.

In the end, I remind you of the devout atmosphere
of our meetings, of your good intentions, your coming
to participate in *Darsul Quran*, your own opinion
about myself and, above all, your well meaning nature,
and I appeal to your clear conscience and upright nature to ponder, for times are critical. Do you see
anywhere the Living Faith which is the ideal of the
Holy Quran, and the sin-consuming fire which the
Holy Quran wants to kindle in the bosoms of men? I
hereby swear by the God of the Great Throne and as-

sure you that this is the very faith that man achieves by entering into *Bai'at* with the Promised Messiah[as]—the vicegerent of the Holy Prophet[sa]—and by keeping his holy company. I am afraid that any delay in this worthy action might cause some terrible change in the heart. Let go the fear of the world, and be prepared to lose everything for the sake of God, so that you may be given everything. *Wassalām.*

> The humble one,
> Abdul Karim
> Qadian
> 1st October, 1898

بِسْمِ اللّٰهِ الرَّحْمٰنِ الرَّحِيْمِ [56]

نَحْمَدُہٗ وَ نُصَلِّیْ عَلٰی رَسُوْلِہِ الْکَرِیْمِ [57]

# Income Tax and a Fresh Sign

صدق را ہر دم مدد آید ز ربّ العلمین        صادقاں را دستِ حق باشد نہاں در آستیں

ہر بلا کز آسماں بر صادقے آید فرود        آخرش گردد نشانے از برائے طالبیں [58]

Some of my foolish opponents were much aggrieved
and frustrated by their failure in the lawsuit started by
Dr. Clark. Despite their every endeavour, they had to
suffer a great defeat in a case in which my life and
honour were at stake. This was not all. The prophecy,
revealed to me regarding the case—that had been
communicated to more than two hundred honourable
and respectable people and had been publicised
widely beforehand—also came to be fulfilled. But,

---

[56] In the name of Allah, the Gracious, the Merciful. **[Publishers]**

[57] We praise Him and invoke blessings upon His noble Prophet[sa].

**Publishers]**

[58] Persian couplet:

*Truth is helped every moment by God, the Sustainer of all*
*the worlds;*
*The truthful have the Hand of the True God concealed in*
*their sleeves.*
*Every calamity that descends from the heavens upon a*
*truthful person,*
*Eventually becomes a sign for the seekers.* **[Publishers]**

unfortunately for my opponents, there was yet another defeat in store for them on account of their suspicious nature and their undue haste. Thus when, recently, in a summary action and without any regular inquiry by any court, this writer was assessed to and notified with a demand to pay income tax to the amount of Rs.187.5, these people, whom it is not necessary to name (the wise will know), greatly rejoiced in their hearts, and thought that though their earlier shot had misfired, they will be compensated for in this case. But evil-minded and selfish people can never triumph. No success can be achieved through one's own cunning or conniving, for there is One Who watches the hearts of men, judges their inner thoughts, and, corresponding to their intentions, issues orders from heaven. God, therefore, did not allow even this desire of these evil-minded people to be fulfilled. After a thorough inquiry, the tax was remitted on 17$^{th}$ September, 1898. The wisdom that lay behind the sudden appearance of this law-suit was that God wished to manifest His support for me in three things and in three aspects, viz. my life, my honour and my property. As far as life and honour were concerned, Divine help had been demonstrated in the case of Dr. Clark, but Divine succour remained to be demonstrated with regard to property. God Almighty, therefore, willed that His support in regard to property should also be

demonstrated to the people. This He did, and in so doing He completed the three forms of succour. This is
the secret behind this lawsuit. Just as God had not
caused Dr. Clark's case to put an end to my life or to
disgrace me—the purpose was to manifest the signs
of the Mighty and Benevolent God—the same was
the case here. And just as in the case involving my
life and honour, God had foretold through revelation
that I would be acquitted and that the opponents
would be humiliated, so did He inform me in advance
that I would be victorious in this case as well and the
envious will be put to shame. And this Divinely revealed prophecy had become well-known in our
Jamāʻat before the final orders had been pronounced.
Just as our Jamāʻat had witnessed a heavenly sign in
the case involving my life and honour, so did they
witness another heavenly sign in this case, which further reinforced their faith. [59] فَالْحَمْدُلِلّٰهِ عَلٰى ذٰلِكَ

I am very much surprised that although sign after
sign continues to appear, the Maulawīs are least concerned with the truth. They do not realize that God
Almighty causes them to suffer defeat in every field.
How they wish that Divine support of some sort or
other should appear in their favour also, but, instead

---

[59] Allah be praised for it. **[Publishers]**

of support, their failure and frustration continues to become apparent with each passing day.

For example, during the days when the almanacs were widely reporting that both the sun and the moon would be eclipsed in the coming month of Ramadan, many people had began to think that perhaps this was the sign of the advent of the Promised Imam. This caused the Maulawīs to fear lest people should incline towards me, for I was the only one claiming to be the Mahdi and the Messiah. In order to conceal this sign, some of them began to proclaim that the eclipse of the sun and the moon would not take place in the coming month of Ramadan, and that it would only take place when their Imam Mahdi appeared. But when the eclipses of the sun and the moon did take place in the month of Ramadan, they started making excuses and saying that these eclipses were not in conformity with the words of Hadith, because the Hadith says that the lunar eclipse would take place on the first night and the solar eclipse on the middle of the month, while in my case, the lunar eclipse took place on the 13th night and the solar eclipse on the 28th of the month. But when it was explained to them that the Hadith did not mean the first night of the moon, as the moon of the first night was not called *Qamar*, but *Hilāl,* and the Hadith contained the word *Qamar* and not *Hilāl.* Therefore, what the Hadith meant was that the moon would be eclipsed on the first of the nights during which lunar eclipse can possibly take place, i.e., 13th night of the moon, and the sun would be eclipsed on the middle one of the days in which it can possibly take place, i.e., the 28th.[60]

After hearing the correct meaning of the Hadith, the ignorant Maulawīs were greatly embarrassed, and came up with yet another excuse saying that one of the narrators of this Hadith was unreliable. It was then pointed out to them that since the prophecy contained in the Hadith had already been fulfilled, any criticism based on mere presumption was of no consequence against the actual facts, which provide a strong proof in favour of the authenticity of the Hadith. In other words, the fulfilment of the prophecy testifies that it is the word of the truthful one. To allege now that he is not truthful but a liar amounts to denying self-

---

[60] According to the laws of nature, lunar eclipse takes place on one of the three appointed nights: The 13th, 14th and 15th [night of the moon]. Eclipse of the moon always takes place on one of these three nights. Thus, in keeping this sequence, the 13th is the first night of the lunar eclipse, to which the Hadith points. As for solar eclipse, the dates are the 27th, 28th and 29th of the [lunar] month. And by this sequence the 28th is the middle one of the dates, and the eclipses took place on these very dates.
**[Author]**

evident truths. Scholars of Hadith have always upheld
the principle that doubt cannot negate certainty. The
fact that this prophecy has been fulfilled literally in
the time of the one who claims to be the Mahdi, is a
sure testimony that he who spoke these words spoke
nothing but the truth. To say that one is not sure of the
character [of the narrator] is only a conjecture, for
sometimes even liars speak the truth. Since the prophecy has also been borne out in other ways and some
leading Hanafite scholars have also testified to it, it
will not only be unfair, but it will be sheer obstinacy
to deny it. After this incontrovertible rejoinder, they
were left with no choice but to admit that the Hadith
was true, and that it was correctly understood to sig-
nify the appearance of the Promised Imam in the near
future; but, they said, this man is not the Promised
Imam, he will be some other person. But this reply of
theirs also proved to be flimsy and false, for had there
been some other Imam, he should have appeared at
the turn of the fourteenth century,[61] as mentioned in
Hadith. But fifteen years of the century have already
passed and no Imam of theirs has yet appeared. The
final excuse they have now come up with is, 'These
people are infidels, don't read their books, and do not

---

[61] According to Islamic calendar known as Hijri calendar.
                                                    **[Publishers]**

have any social relations with them. Do not listen to them, for what they say moves the hearts.' It should serve as a warning for them that the heaven has turned against them and so has the earth at the present time. How shameful it is that while the heaven is testifying against them on the one hand, the earth too has turned against them on account of the dominance of the Cross. The testimony of the heavens—the prophecy regarding the solar and lunar eclipses during Ramadan—is recorded in books such as *Dār Quṭnī.* And the testimony of the earth is the supremacy of the Cross, during which the Promised Messiah was destined to come, and this Hadith figures in *Ṣaḥīḥ Bukhārī.* Both these testimonies favour us and reject them.

The death of Lekhram[62] was also a sign that caused them no less mortification.

My paper that was read out at the *Mahutsu*[63] convention—the conference of religions—was acclaimed as a great sign, and caused my opponents no little embarrassment. It was not just that my paper pre-

---

[62] Pundit Lekhram: An Ārya Samāj leader from Peshawar. **[Publishers]**
[63] *Mahutsu*: Conference held in Lahore Dec. 1896, in which the Promised Messiah's[as] paper was universally acclaimed. **[Publishers]**

vailed over all others, but this victory had been foretold in a prophecy that had been published earlier in
an announcement.

If only Atham[64] had lived, Miyān Muhammad
Husain Batalvi and his ilk would have some reason to
indulge in some false interpretations, but Atham, with
his hasty death, was the undoing of these people. He
lived as long as he kept quiet, but the moment he
opened his mouth he was overtaken by the condition
stipulated in the revelation. God Almighty granted
him respite in keeping with the conditions laid down
in the revelation, but the moment he violate this condition, he was seized with terrible illness and it
quickly put an end to his life. But since some of the
ignorant Maulawīs remained impervious to this humiliation, and, out of sheer mischief, regarded the
conditional prophecy as if it was wholly unconditional, they did not draw any honest conclusion from
the obvious panic and silence which had taken hold of
Atham during the time specified in the prophecy. Nor
did they draw any lesson from the fact that I invited
Atham to take an oath, and he was also incited [by his

---

[64] Abdullah Atham: A prominent Christian cleric and preacher,
who in his book *Andrūna-e-Bible* used vile language against
the Holy Prophet[sa]. **[Publishers]**

supporters] to file a suit against me, but he would not hear of these things. Since, God does not wish to let His signs to languish in ambiguity, He caused the prophecy about Lekhram to be fulfilled with unmistakable clarity. The prophecy was unconditional, and contained all the details about the date, the day and the manner of his death. But alas! the enemies of truth did not profit even from this manifest sign of God. It is evident that if I was a liar, the prophecy about Lekhram would have been a great occasion to humiliate me, for it had no condition attached to it, and I had published a written statement along with the prophecy that if it turned out to be false, I should be considered a liar deserving every punishment and humiliation. On this occasion, if I had been a liar, God Almighty would surely have disgraced me and wiped out every trace of me and my Jamā'at. But He did not do so. Rather, He manifested my honour and enlightened the hearts of those who, on account of their ignorance, had not understood the prophecy about Atham. Is it not a point to ponder as to why God supported me in the matter of a prophecy that had no condition attached to it, and non fulfilment of which would have meant my total ruin? Why did He fulfil this prophecy and thereby fill hundreds of hearts with my love—so much so that some of my sworn enemies came to me crying and entered into my *Bai'at*? Had this prophecy not been fulfilled, Miyān Batalvi Sahib may well imagine what forceful articles he would have published in *Ishā'atus Sunna* against me, and what effect they would have had on the people. Can anyone understand why God should have heaped shame and disgrace on Batalvi and his ilk, and has it not been decreed in the Holy Quran that God shall always grant victory to the believers? And what would have been left of me, if this prophecy—which was not accompanied by any condition whatsoever, and related to an opponent who would gnash his teeth at me—had turned out to be false? Is it not true that if this prophecy had turned out to be false, Shaikh Muhammad Husain Batalvi would have leapt with joy? He would have written gleeful articles in his paper, poking ridicule and fun at me, and would have held public celebrations. But, what has he done now that the prophecy has been fulfilled? Is it not true that he has thrown away a great Divine sign as though it was rubbish, and has insinuated in his blighted paper that I am the murderer of Lekhram! Yes, I am a killer, but I do not kill with man-made weapons, rather I kill with a heavenly weapon—i.e., prayer, and I had to resort to this only due to his insistence and repeated requests. I did not wish to pray against him, but he himself desired it. I can be accused of murder in the same way as the Holy Prophet[sa] was accused in the case of Khusro Parvez, the King of Persia.

Thus, Lekhram's case clinched the Divine argument against Muhammad Husain and others like him.

Thereafter came the Divine sign relating to the lawsuit initiated by Dr. Clark, and the prophecy, which had been publicised widely among hundreds of people before the judgement was announced, was fulfilled. Shaikh Batalvi suffered such disgrace in this case that, had he been fortunate enough, he would have repented at once, for it had become evident to him as to who enjoyed Divine support.

Remember that in Clark's case, Muhammad Husain in collusion with the Christians, had spared no effort to disgrace me. My God acquitted me, but he suffered such humiliation when he asked for a chair in the court, that any decent person in his place could have died of shame. This is what comes of trying to humiliate a truthful person. On his demand for a chair, the Deputy Commissioner rebuked him and said, 'Neither you nor your father have ever been entitled to a chair.' He ordered him to move back and stand straight. What was even worse, as he was being snubbed, I, whose disgrace he had come to witness, was seated on a chair close to the Deputy Commissioner. I will not keep repeating this incident. If anyone wants, he can go and confirm it from the officials of the court and their staff.

Now the question is, while God Almighty promises in the Holy Quran that He supports the believers and gives them honour, and that He disgraces the liars, then why is there this contradiction that in every field, disgrace, notoriety and dishonour have been the lot of Muhammad Husain? Is this the way God treats those whom He loves? As to the income tax case, it was Shaikh Batalvi's earnest wish that tax should somehow be imposed on me, so that he could embellish the pages of his magazine *Ishā'atus Sunna* by writing about it, and thus cover up, at least to some extent, his earlier humiliations. However, in this too he failed miserably and the tax was remitted. God had placed the case in the hands of officials who were going to do justice in all truth and fairness. Thus the unlucky ill-wishers were frustrated in this case as well. God be thanked a thousand times that He revealed the truth to the authorities. Here, I should thank Mr. T. Dixon, Deputy Commissioner, District Gurdaspur, to whom God Almighty disclosed the facts. This is the reason why, from the very beginning, I have been grateful to the British Government and its officials, and have been all praise for them because they always uphold justice. Both Captain Douglas, the former Commissioner, [in Dr. Clarke's case], and Mr. T. Dixon [in

the income tax case], have provided us with two ex-
amples of British justice and fairness that I can't
forget as long as I live. For instance, the case before
Captain Douglas was a very sensitive one, in which
the complainant was a venerable Christian, and he
was supported by almost all the Christian clergy in
the Punjab. But the aforesaid Commissioner did not
care, who had initiated the case. Instead he acted with
justice and acquitted me. The case heard by Mr. T.
Dixon was also very sensitive, for the government
suffers loss in remitting a tax. But Mr. Dixon acted
with the utmost regard for fairness, justice and equity.
To my mind, such officials are a shining example of
the government's concern for its citizens, and of its
honesty and adherence to the principles of justice.
And that which was comprehended by Mr. T. Dixon's
enlightened sense of justice was indeed the truth. I
am, therefore full of gratitude and prayer. The hard
work and investigation done by Munshi Taj-ud-Din,
Tehsildar Batala, also deserves mention here. It was he
who, in his spirit of justice and earnest investigation,
presented a true picture of the facts before the higher
officials, and this helped them to arrive at the truth.
Here I reproduce the Tehsildar's report and the final order issued by the Deputy Commissioner:

> Copy of the Report by Munshi Taj-ud-Din Sahib,
> Tehsildar, Pargana Batala, District Gurdaspur, in Tax

Objection case.

Attached to file in the court of Mr. T. Dixon, Deputy Commissioner. Date of institution: 20th June, 1898. Decided: 17th September, 1898. Basta No from Department: Case No. 55/46.

Income Tax Objection filed by Mirza Ghulam Ahmad, son of Ghulam Murtaza, caste Mughal, resident of Qadian, Tehsil Batala, District Gurdaspur.

**To The Deputy Commissioner, Gurdaspur**

Sir,

Mirza Ghulam Ahmad of Qadian was assessed this year to pay income tax to the amount of Rs. 187.5. No tax has ever been imposed upon Mirza Ghulam Ahmad before. Since it was a new tax, Mirza Ghulam Ahmad filed objections in your court which were referred to this department for inquiry. Before referring to the inquiry regarding the income tax, it would be appropriate to say something about Mirza Ghulam Ahmad of Qadian, to find out who and of what status is the petitioner.

Mirza Ghulam Ahmad belongs to an old and noble Mughal family which has been residing in the village of Qadian for a long time. His father, Mirza Ghulam Murtaza was a respectable landlord and the Chief of Qadian. On his death, he left an estate of quite sizeable proportions, a part of which is still in the possession of Mirza Ghulam Ahmad, and a part thereof is with Mirza Sultan Ahmad, son of Ghulam Ahmad, which he has inherited through the wife of the late Mirza Ghulam Qadir. This estate is largely agricultural. It consists, for example, of an orchard, cultivated land, and *Ta'alluqadārī* of a few villages. As Mirza Ghulam Murtaza was a respectable and affluent person, it is possible, and in my opinion quite probable, that he left a large amount of cash and jewellery, but satisfying evidence in regard to this kind of immovable[65] property is not available. Mirza Ghulam Ahmad himself has been in service in his early days, and, in view of his lifestyle, it cannot be expected that he might have squandered away his own income or his father's estate, cash, or ornaments. Immovable property, which he inherited from his father, is still intact, but regarding immovable[66] assets, sufficient evidence could not be procured. In any case, taking into consideration Mirza Ghulam Ahmad's circumstances, it can be safely said that he has not wasted these assets either. Some time ago, Mirza Ghulam Ahmad relinquished his post and devoted his attention to religion, consistently endeavouring to have himself recognized as head of a religious Jamā'at. He has published several religious books, written pamphlets

---

[65] It seems to be a misprint. To be read as moveable **[Publishers]**
[66] Ibid

and given publicity to his views through announcements. The result of all this is that for some time now, a sect consisting of a number of individuals, of whom a list (in English) is attached herewith, has come to believe in him as their leader, and they have established themselves as a separate sect which, according to the list attached, comprises 318 persons. Some of them, though not many, belong to the nobility and are highly educated. When his Jamāʻat grew in number, he made an appeal for subscription to his followers in his books entitled *Fatḥ-e-Islam* and *Tauḍīḥ-e-Marām* in order to provide means to achieve his objectives, mentioning five items for which funds were required. As his followers reposed their full trust in him, they gradually started sending subscriptions, at times specifying in their letters the particular item, out of the five, towards which they wished their subscription to be spent. Sometimes they left it to Mirza Ghulam Ahmad's discretion to spend on whichever item he thought proper. The statement of Mirza Ghulam Ahmad, the complainant, and the evidence of other witnesses shows that the money is being spent in the aforesaid manner. In short, this Jamāʻat at present exists as a religious society whose head is Mirza Ghulam Ahmad. All the rest are his followers who fulfil the objectives of the Jamāʻat on a cooperative basis through their subscriptions. The five items mentioned above are as follows:

1. The Guest house: All who come to Qadian to meet Mirza Ghulam Ahmad, whether they are his followers or not, but who have come for religious enquiry are provided food from this guest house. According to the written statement of Mirza Ghulam Ahmad's attorney, the funds allocated for this purpose are also spent for the welfare of travellers, orphans and widows.

2. The Press: Religious books and handbills are printed here, which are at times distributed free to the public.

3. The School: The followers of Mirza Ghulam Ahmad have established a school, which is still in its early stages. Its management is under Maulawī Nur-ud-din who is a prominent follower of Mirza Ghulam Ahmad.

4: Annual Conventions: The Jamā'at holds annual conventions, and subscriptions are collected for organizing them.

5. Correspondence: According to the written statement of Mirza Ghulam Ahmad's attorney and the evidence of witnesses, a considerable amount of money is spent for this purpose. Members of the

Jamāʿat contribute towards the cost of all correspondence in connection with religious enquiries.

In short, according to the statements of witnesses, subscriptions are expended on these five items. These are the ways and means by which Mirza Ghulam Ahmad, along with his followers, disseminates his religious views. This society is a religious denomination, and since your honour already knows about it, this brief outline should suffice.

I now proceed to the actual petition.

The annual income of Mirza Ghulam Ahmad this year, having been assessed at Rs.7200/-, was taxed to the amount of Rs. 187.5.[67] On his request, his statement was taken at Qadian, while I was on tour in that area. Statements of 13 witnesses were recorded. Mirza Ghulam Ahmad deposed in his affidavit that he had income from his *Taʿalluqadārī*, from his land and from his orchard: *Taʿalluqadārī* income being about 82 rupees and 10 annas per annum; income from land about 300 rupees per annum, and from the orchard about two, three, four or, at the most, five hundred rupees per annum. He has no other income of any kind apart from this. Mirza Ghulam Ahmad also deposed

---

[67] 187 rupees and 8 annas, or 187.5 rupees. **[Publishers]**

that this year he had received about Rs. 5200/- from his followers, whereas the average income is about Rs. 4000/- which is spent solely on the five above mentioned items, and not on his person. No regular income and expenditure account has been kept and the approximate estimate as stated is only given from memory. Mirza Ghulam Ahmad further stated that his personal income from the orchard, the land and *Ta'alluqadārī* was sufficient for his personal expenses and that he had no need to expend his followers' money on his own person. Statements of witnesses also support Mirza Ghulam Ahmad's deposition. It is stated that his followers send money to Mirza Ghulam Ahmad by way of charitable donations to be spent on the five above mentioned heads and is accordingly expended. Mirza Ghulam Ahmad has no personal income that might be taxable except that from *Ta'alluqadārī*, his land and his orchard. Of the witnesses, six are reliable, but they are his followers who live with him most of the time. Seven other witnesses are shopkeepers who have no relation of any kind with Mirza Sahib. All these witnesses generally support Mirza Ghulam Ahmad's statement. They affirm that Mirza Ghulam Ahmad has no other personal income except from *Ta'alluqadārī*, his land and his orchard. I also inquired secretly from some of people in that place regarding the personal income of Mirza Ghulam

Ahmad. Although some of them did say that Mirza
Ghulam Ahmad's personal income was considerable
and that it was taxable, no one was able to provide any
clear evidence. I also visited the school and the guest
house in Qadian. The school is still in an early stage
and is largely built of mud. Some houses have also
been built for the followers. There were guests in the
guest house, and I noted that all the followers who
were present in Qadian on that day had their meals in
the guest house.

In my humble opinion, if Mirza Ghulam Ahmad's
personal income is taken to derive from *Ta'alluqadārī*
and his orchard alone—as is clear form the evidence,
and the income from his followers is regarded as
charitable contribution, then the tax imposed on
Mirza Ghulam Ahmad cannot be upheld. On the other
hand, when we consider that Mirza Ghulam Ahmad
comes of a respected and influential family and his
ancestors have been important chiefs with substantial
incomes, and that Mirza Ghulam Ahmad himself has
been in service and in comfortable circumstances, one
tends to imagine that Mirza Ghulam Ahmad is a rich
person and is, therefore, liable to tax. According to
Mirza Sahib's own statement, he has recently mort-
gaged his garden to his wife and has received in return
ornaments worth Rs. 4000/- and Rs 1000/- in cash. A
man whose wife can afford to spare such an amount can

be thought of as being rich. The whole record of the inquiry conducted by me is enclosed with this file. I beg leave to submit this report in compliance with your orders. Dated: 31st August, 1898.

The humble one, Taj-ud-Din, Tehsildar, Batala, submits that the attorney for Mirza Ghulam Ahmad has been directed to appear in your court on 3rd September, 1898. Dated as above, under official signature.

Copy of interim order on Tax Objection, filed in the court of T. Dixon, Deputy Commissioner, Distt. Gurdaspur.

File Income Tax Objection : Mirza Ghulam Ahmad, son of Ghulam Murtaza, caste Mughal, resident of Qadian, Tehsil Batala, Distt. Gurdaspur.

Papers seen and report of the Tehsildar heard today. For the time being this file is to be kept under consideration. Shaikh Ali Ahmad, pleader and attorney for the appellant are present and are informed. Dated: 3rd September, 1898.

Under official signature.

Here I reproduce the original copy of the final orders [English] along with the Urdu translation:

In the court of F.T. Dixon Esquire, Collector of the District of Gurdaspur.

Income Tax objection case No. 46 of 1898. Mirza Ghulam Ahmad son of Mirza Ghulam Murtaza, caste Mughal, resident of mauda Qadian Mughlan, Tehsil Batala, Distt. of Gurdaspur objector.

### Order

This tax is a newly imposed one and Mirza Ghulam Ahmad claims that all his income is applied not to his personal but to the expenses of sect he has founded. He admits that he has other property but he stated to the Tehsildar that even the proceeds of that which is classed as land and the proceeds of agriculture and is exempt under 5 (b) go to his religious expenses. I see no reason to doubt the bona fides of this man, whose sect is well known, and I exempt his income from subscriptions which he states as 5200/- Under Sec 5(c) as being solely employed in religious purposes.

Sd T. Dixon
Collector
17-9-1898

# Index

## A

Abdul Karim, Maulawī — 48, 55, 60
's letter to a friend — 55
came to stay in Qadian — 56
used to deliver sermons — 57
Adam — 55
*Akhbār-e-'Ām* — 35
Alexander of Rome — 16
Ali Ahmad, Shaikh — 81
*Al-Mu'aṭṭa* — 40
Amir Ali Shah, Sayyid — 50
*Andrūna-e-Bible*
a book by Atham — 68
Arabia — 9, 28
Ārya Samāj — 67
Atham — 68
died in accordance with the revelation — 68
Atheism
denial of revelation has turned millions of Hindus as, — 34
*Awāriful M'ārif* — 58

## B

Baba Nanak — 35
*Bai'at*
object of, is to acquire spiritual knowledge, blessings and signs — 44
true concept of, — 44
Balaam — 4, 9, 19
parished when confronted Moses[as] — 19
*Walī* of his time — 19
Bible — 28
*Brāhīn-e-Ahmadiyya* — 51
Brahmo Samāj
deny revelation — 31

## C

*Chola Sahib*
verses of the Holy Quran are inscribed on — 35
Clark, Dr. — 61, 62, 63, 71

## D

Damascus — 40
*Dār Quṭnī* — 67
Death of Jesus[as]
Imam Malik, Ibn Hazm and Mu'tazilites believed in — 41
the verse فَلَمَّاتَوَفَّيْتَنِيْ proves, — 41
Divine Signs
four kinds of, given to the Promised Messiah[as] — 42
sign of Dr. Clark — 71
sign of Hajj — 43
sign of Lekhram — 69
sign of plague — 43
sign of solar and lunar eclipse — 43
Douglas, Captain — 73
Judge in Dr. Clark's case — 72
Promised Messiah[as] praised, — 72

## E

Eclipse
appointed dates for lunar and solar, — 65
fulfilment of the prophecy of, removes all criticism — 65
Hadith of, has been testified by Hanafite scholars — 66
Hadith of, recorded in *Dār Quṭnī* — 67
lunar and solar, a sign for the Promised Messiah[as] — 64

83

absorption of, in God is more profound
than that of all the *Auliyā'* — 19
hallmarks of, — 10
his end is woeful who does not
recognize the, — 5
is like a Sun — 36
not appointed by God are not, — 39
outcome of the spiritual radiation
which comes with, — 6
revelations of, are extremely useful in
strengthening the belief — 20
term, comprises all Prophets,
Messengers, *Muḥaddathīn* and
*Mujaddadīn* — 39
the Promised Messiah's[as] claim 'I am
the Imam of the Age' — 39
was to appear at the turn of the 14th
century as mentioned in Hadith —
66
Imāmat
faculty of, is ingrained in the nature of
Imam — 14
Income Tax Case — 61
a heavenly sign — 63
manifested God's support for the
Promised Messiah's[as] life, honour
and property — 62
order written by T. Dixon — 81
Promised Messiah[as] was notified to
pay Rs.187.5 — 62
report submitted by Munshi Taj-ud-
Din Sahib, Tehsildar Batala — 73
tax was remitted on 17th September,
1898 — 62
India — 40
*Ishā'atus Sunna* — 72
Miyān Batalwi sahib would publish
forceful articles in, against the
Promised Messiah[as] — 70

# J

Jains
reject Vedas — 34

Jerusalem — 40
Jesus[as] — 8, 11, 22, 25, 26, 27, 29, 32,
39
harsh words used by, were not out of
fit of anger or frenzy — 11
not every saint or sufi can repel Satan's
suggestion as, did — 27
one gospel says, did not die on the
cross — 24
Satan could not stand up against, —
26
some evengalists mistakenly thought
that, had died on the cross — 24
temptation by devil was a spiritual
conversation — 23
Jewish Scholars
before the advent of the Holy
Prophet[as] godly, after receiving
revelation immigrated to Arabia —
9
self-conciet kept most of, from
accepting the Holy Prophet[sa] — 9
thousands of, perished when confronted
the Holy Prophet[sa] — 20

# K

Khalsas
reject Vedas — 35
*Khātamul Ambiyā'* — 8

# L

Lahore — 50, 67
Leiah — 50
Lekhram — 67, 69, 71
Muhammad Husain Batalwi accused
the Promised Messiah[as] of
murdering, — 70
Love for God
the Promised Messiah[as] writes
'no one can equal me in my,' — 52